MW00886205

# POLARIZED

### The Case for Civility in the Time of Trump
### – An experiment in civil discourse on Facebook

Jeff Rasley
Midsummer Books
Indianapolis, Indiana
Copyright 2017 by Jeff Rasley

ISBN-13: 978-1548407698
ISBN-10: 1548407690

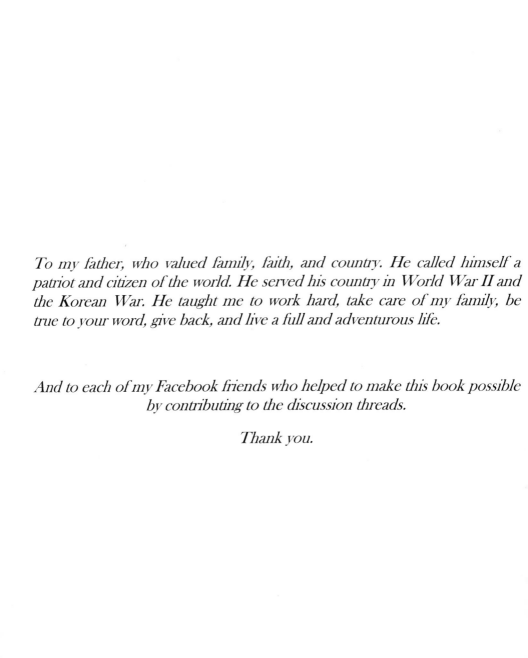

*To my father, who valued family, faith, and country. He called himself a patriot and citizen of the world. He served his country in World War II and the Korean War. He taught me to work hard, take care of my family, be true to your word, give back, and live a full and adventurous life.*


*And to each of my Facebook friends who helped to make this book possible by contributing to the discussion threads.*

*Thank you.*

# Table of Contents

# Introduction

*An Experiment in Facebook*

**The claims:**

1. Political polarization has become so widespread and deep that the civic health of the nation is at risk.
2. The way social media is used contributes to an unhealthy political polarization.

**The issues:**

1. Can Facebook be a medium to reduce political polarization?
2. Or, is it designed to tempt users to express themselves impulsively and angrily about political issues?
3. And, does Facebook encourage users to avoid interacting with people of different political alignments than their own?

**An experiment to find the answers:**

A month after Donald Trump's inauguration I asked my FB friends whether they were willing to engage in civil discussions about current political issues. Most answered negatively. They did not want to interact with people "on the other side". The animosity generated by the Clinton v. Trump presidential election drove many of my FB friends into silos of the "like-minded". They wanted to stay there.

I went ahead with the experiment anyway. I posted statements and questions about issues ranging from immigration to terrorism and abortion. I asked for comments from friends across the political spectrum, from rightwing evangelical Christians to leftwing socialists. I requested the participants to be civil and respectful toward those with whom they disagreed.

**Conclusion:** It worked (sort of).

# I. The State of Political Discourse in Social Media

*Anger may be defined as an impulse, accompanied by pain, to a conspicuous revenge for a conspicuous slight directed without justification towards what concerns oneself or towards what concerns one's friends. ... Hence it has been well said about wrath,*
*Sweeter it is by far than the honeycomb dripping with sweetness,*
*And spreads through the hearts of men.*
Aristotle's ***Rhetoric***, Book II, Chapter 2

The 21st Century technology of social media brings out the primitive pre-homo sapien instinct of fight or flight in us users. It tempts us to attack anyone who confronts or offends. It offers us sanctuary from attack in privacy settings and closed groups.

## Angry Political Rants vs. Narcissic Blather on Facebook

After the election of Barak Obama in 2008 I occasionally noticed angry posts by Facebook friends about the President. These were not rational arguments critical of Obama's policies. They were attacks against his person. Nasty and mean-spirited posts about Obama became more common after his re-election in 2012. During the 2016 presidential primaries these same angry FB friends turned their guns on Hillary Clinton. Anti-Trump FB friends began responding in kind. After Trump's election, my notifications of Facebook posts turned into a tsunami of fury directed against President Trump.

The increase in angry and unrefined outbursts I was experiencing with Facebook was a microcosm of mounting polarizing political hatred in the US. You might ask, so what if people use Facebook and other social media to vent their rage against politicians they dislike and their supporters? What's the harm in that? Considered in isolation, perhaps there is no harm. But as a symptom of a disease in our body politic, it is evidence that we have become sick.

According to the Pew Research Center, "A majority of Americans now say they get news via social media, and half of the public has turned to these sites to learn about the 2016 presidential election." Pew Research Center, "Social Media Update 2016," November 11, 2016. We don't just hoot and bellow our political frustrations on social media; we increasingly turn to it for information to develop our own political opinions. Logging on to a social media network has consequences.

I joined Facebook in 2008, the year Barack Obama was elected President. Early on I noticed that a few friends regularly posted serious political commentary with links to relevant articles. Discussion threads about political issues occasionally developed among my FB friends. Reasoned arguments and counter-arguments were posted and commented on in some of these threads. When someone posted a link to an article about, for example, the proposed bailout of GM, comments followed and arguments developed through replies. My recollection is that these threads appeared more frequently than the occasional ad hominem attack against President Obama.

Before Obama's reelection in 2012 the quantity of political posts by my FB friends, including the rants and reasoned discussions, was minuscule compared to the garden variety of Facebook posts about coffee and food, travel and pet photos, deaths and births of loved ones, engagements, entertainment-oriented articles, silly YouTube videos, baby pictures, art projects, etc. But the trickle of political posts turned into a stream after Obama's reelection in 2012. The frequency of discussion-type threads did not increase. What increased were mean-spirited comments about President Obama. Some of my Republican FB friends were so irked that Obama beat Romney they just couldn't let it go.

The ugly posts about Obama didn't invite thoughtful responses. The obvious purpose was to malign the President or to let off steam by friends who really disliked Obama. The anti-Obama venting rarely generated many responses. A few "likes" and one or two even nastier comments might follow. An Obama supporter or two might reply with a rude comment about the original post or the friend who posted it. I can remember one friend publicly unfriending another as a result of a quarrel over nasty posts about Obama.

Rudeness and nastiness on Facebook became even more the norm after Donald Trump began winning primaries in the 2016 presidential campaign. The regular stream of angry anti-Obama posts was a minor tributary compared to the deluge of anti-Trump posts that appeared before and after the 2016 elections. Clinton was also pilloried, but the quantity of anti-Clinton posts within my network was significantly lower than those aimed at Trump. The nastiness was not just directed at Trump and Clinton. It targeted their supporters as well.

The fury expressed by my anti-Trump friends toward pro-Trumpers is exemplified in this comment posted in response to my invitation to FB friends to participate in "experimental civil discussion threads about political issues".

> ... I have no internal curiosity to understand their motivation nor the need to feel fair and balanced. I am 59 years old and have earned my right to be opinionated. I am not at all embarrassed by or ashamed of it. I'm tolerant of a whole lot of things. Child molesters and Trump supporters are not among them.

C_ is not ashamed, she's proud of her intolerance of Trump supporters. It's understandable that you would want nothing to do with people you equate with child molesters. So, what's the likelihood of success in trying to promote civil discourse about political issues in this climate of angry intolerance? Pretty low, it would seem.

One way to find out whether members of opposing political camps would even be willing to try to engage in civil conversations about political issues was to give it a try on my own Facebook page. The interesting result of that endeavor is what inspired this book.

I have written and taught a class at two different universities about the value of promoting cross-cultural tolerance and understanding. The theme I've pursued is summarized in this passage from a previous book, *Godless – Living a Valuable Life beyond Beliefs*:

> The way forward toward a more peaceful world and harmonious communities is letting go of divisive beliefs and ideologies. Instead of trying to live according to a prescribed set of beliefs, we should try to guide our lives with positive values. Beliefs divide us into believers, those with different beliefs, and unbelievers. Values unite us in shared aspirations to become better persons living in better communities.

> Most people in most cultures and countries share a similar set of fundamental values. That's why people of differing backgrounds generally get along with each other. Notice how diverse people from all over the planet speaking different languages manage to negotiate the sidewalks in Manhattan, Paris, or Tokyo without pushing, shoving, or any significant violence. Most of us most of the time practice the value of respecting other people's physical space.

> Divisions arise and trouble begins when religious doctrines or political ideologies are more important than valuing Tolerance and Consideration for others. Caring more about the abstract ideas and beliefs of religions and political parties than about people has caused much pain and suffering in the world.

To try to promote civil conversations involving pro and anti Trump friends I invited them to participate in discussion threads about political issues on my Facebook page. Given the animosity between these two camps, I was not optimistic. I was hopeful.

I originally joined Facebook at the invitation of Sarah (names are changed throughout), a childhood friend, who was trying to reconnect with old friends who'd fallen out of touch. Facebook quickly became a pleasant diversion from a busy life. Like Sarah, I sought out people I'd lost touch with and built up a community of several hundred friends within a year or so. I enjoyed checking in on a regular basis to see what was up with people I rarely saw in person.

On a more meaningful level, Facebook was a vessel of solace after the death of my father. I posted a death notice on my page. Over 300 friends expressed their care, concerns, thoughts, and prayers for my family and me. Many others clicked the emoticon for grief. To cynics, a comment of sympathy in social media might seem superficial. I found it comforting just to learn that so many FB friends would do so.

However, on a typical day when I logged onto my FB page the experience began to change during the presidential campaign in 2012. It was more harrowing, and more interesting, because of political posts during the Obama/Romney race for the presidency. Since then, notifications of angry and ugly political commentaries have competed for my attention with pleasant and narcissic blather. After the 2016 election of Donald Trump, the furious posting by progressive-Democrat friends made the Tea-Party anti-Obama friends look like pikers. I have received daily notifications of at least twenty anti-Trump posts from a single FB friend ever since the election was final. I am writing this sentence months after Trump was sworn in, but my zealous friend has not slacked off.

I messaged Greg that I was worried his obsessive anti-Trump posting on Facebook was becoming pathological. He replied that he was committed to "long term resistance". I don't fault Greg for his political commitment. I applaud him for being so engaged. What I question is the way he is using Facebook to try to achieve his political objective. Is a daily stream of anti-Trump posts on Facebook an effective way to 'resist" the policies of the Trump administration? Wouldn't his time be better spent as suggested in an April 26, 2017 article in *Slate*, "The Moderate's Case Against Trump", by William Saletan.

> You don't have to hate Donald Trump to see he is bad at his job... You don't have to stand for it. Call your senators and your member of Congress. Demand better health care and a fairer tax system. Go to their town halls. Tell them to oppose Trump when he doesn't do what's right for the country. If they don't listen to you, organize and vote them out next year.

From my vantage point, Greg's most significant accomplishment has been to alienate many of his FB friends. Most of Greg's anti-Trump friends tired of the daily deluge of his posts. He completely alienated all of the pro-Trump friends he had. One long-time friend of Greg's, who is a Trump supporter, made it a point of pride to regularly reply to Greg's posts. After several months she finally went quiet after a last reply telling Greg to "accept reality". Greg does have a couple friends who respond to some of his posts. But that number has dwindled dramatically from when he first began his campaign.

The net effect of Greg's unceasing attacks on Facebook against the President and his supporters is that he and one or two of his friends daily vent their shared fury that Trump won the 2016 election. They are changing no minds. They are not even communicating with anyone who disagrees with them.

Greg is the most prolific, but several other FB friends typically post at least a couple angry or snarky anti-Trump blasts every day. A couple random examples:

May 24 at 2:51pm. The conversation went something like this:
Russian official: $$$$$$$$$$$$?
Trump adviser: Yes, $$$$$$$$$$$$$, and $$$$$$$$ for me.

May 16 at 6:15pm. I doubt there is anything that will sway Trump supporters- not bragging about trying to f*** a married woman, grabbing women's p*****s, admitting he was thinking about Russia when he fired Comey- the man heading up the Russian Investigation, admitting in a tweet he had a right to discuss classified information with the Russians (basically admitting that he did it). What does Trump have to do before they realize he is unfit for office?

I still receive numerous daily notices of posts by FB friends about their pets, parents, children, trips, and favorite foods. But a huge (as President Trump would say) proportion of the notices of posts I have received since the election are one-sided pissed-off diatribes against Trump.

When the use of Facebook for political posting by friends first began trending, it interested and excited me. Wow! I didn't know that June, who I hadn't seen since high school graduation, was a right-wing evangelical Obama-hater. I wondered whether Paul, who I'd lost touch with after college, had moderated his Marxism with age. It was interesting to learn that he thought Sanders would be a fiscal disaster and was supporting Clinton.

My enjoyment began to wane as the fevered pitch of the posts increased and the opportunity for conversation and rational discourse decreased. During the later Obama years political posts by my friends began to resemble boxing matches more than reasoned discussions. Instead of comments and replies about a significant event or issue, verbal punches were being thrown. The punches usually missed in the sense that comments tended to come from fellow travelers who wanted to pile on with even nastier replies. Sometimes an Obama supporter struck back. But these exchanges were not reasoned arguments. They were attacks and counter-attacks (like, "Jane, you ignorant slut!" for those of a certain age).

Bearing witness to the trading of insults and ridicule, and occasionally giving in to the temptation to hurl a barb myself, began to lose its thrill and became increasingly disturbing to me by the time Donald Trump was inaugurated President of the United States.

I was unsettled by the election of Donald Trump. I voted for Clinton and expected, like most Americans, she would win. Was howling in rage about my disappointment the best way to use my social media networks? Did it help to move the country forward in any way by insulting and ridiculing friends who are Trump supporters, or to unfriend them? I didn't think so. But for awhile I didn't know what else to do. I was not alone.

I found myself wishing for a return to those early days of my FB use, untroubled by political rants and pleasantly enjoying photos of a friend's travel excursions and a cat video.

### *Political Posts on Facebook; its Highest (or lowest) and Best (or worst) Use*

As the shock of Trump's victory wore off I began to tire of the unceasing outpouring of anger by disappointed Clinton voters. Weren't my friends and I wasting a valuable resource? Surely there is a higher and better use of social media networks than insulting political opponents or posting cat videos. Instead of contributing to the polarization of disappointed Clinton supporters versus triumphant Trump supporters, could we use Facebook as a medium to try to find some common ground on important issues plaguing our nation? Could Facebook be a place of healing in a divided country? At the very least, couldn't we use it as a means to better understand those who voted differently than we did?

Maybe; maybe not.

Perhaps Facebook is maturing (or degenerating) into a new phase of use, which has coincided with the polarization of the American people. FB users may have grown tired of the sometimes pleasant and often narcissic expressions typically posted on Facebook. They might enjoy being juiced with outrage at a political post that infuriates them. We might need to let off steam about the stupid things our politicians do. Social media is a perfect venue for getting high with rage and then letting it out. It doesn't actually hurt anyone, does it?

Using Facebook for political purposes does make it a more meaningful experience. The increasing anger of political posts, dating back to the 2012 presidential campaign, reflects the rising temperature within the country. Not due to climate change, but due to the swell of animosity toward Barak Obama by the Tea Party movement and then the fury of progressive liberals over the election of Donald Trump. "You don't have to be a weatherman to know which way the wind blows," to have seen the political storm rising. Just open your Facebook page or check out your Twitter feed. The reality of an angry, divided nation smacked you in the face whenever you logged onto either social network.

There are benefits that have come from this trend of angry political posting. It is an avenue to vent. Isn't it good for our mental and emotional health to let it out and release our anger?

Yes, to a point; but words can hurt. People get hurt enough on Facebook that they unfriend each other. And that's not healthy.

Okay, so another benefit might be that you can learn where your friends line up politically. It was interesting to satisfy my curiosity about which candidates and party my old friends June and Paul support. With that kind of intelligence about our FB friends we have a better sense of what topics to avoid and how to slant our comments, if we don't' want to piss off those friends.

That benefit can also be a detriment. Why should we tiptoe around political issues? Wouldn't the virtual world be more habitable if we honestly expressed ourselves about political issues?

But that requires a commitment to civility and tolerance of disagreement. Otherwise, political posts inevitably turn into rants and insult trading.

If your typical experience of political-oriented posts was meaningful only to the extent that you learned a friend was outraged about something Romney, Obama, Clinton, or Trump did, how valuable is that? If your own posts are expressions of ridicule at the stupidity of those who support politicians you can't stand, how much value are you getting from the time spent writing those tweets or comments?

Rage is not a healthy state of being to marinate in. Heart rate and blood pressure increase, and body temperature actually rises. Being "hot", not sexually attractive, but hot with anger is an accurate description of the physiological response to a stimulus which angers us. If anger is sustained for long periods, or is experienced too frequently, it can cause a stroke or heart attack.

> Anger is hostile to understanding. At its most implacable or extreme, it prevents comprehension of a situation, of the people you oppose, of your own role and responsibilities. It's not for nothing that we call rages "blind".
> Rebecca Solnit, *Harper's Magazine*, "Easy Chair", May 2017

Solnit claims that in social media anger is the go to emotion. "On social media, audiences give perfunctory attention to facts so that they can move on to the pleasure of righteous wrath about the latest person who has said or done something wrong."

Users of social media should ask: Is that all there is?

The experiment I eventually performed on my Facebook page was aspirational – to try to achieve a higher and better use. My Facebook page could become a forum for friends with different political leanings to engage in civil discourse about important political issues. Instead of posting rude and hostile comments about political foes, we could try to better understand those on the other side of the political chasm. Alignments might not change, but we'd have a better understanding of why those we disagree with take the positions that they do.

An increased level of understanding through civil conversation is the best – probably the only -- way to reduce the toxic polarization of our politics. However, expecting that to occur in any venue, especially in social media, in the time of Trump would require a strong dose of optimism.

Marinating in my own rage over Trump's election had lost its appeal. By the time he was inaugurated President I wanted to do something more useful than expressing shock or outrage. An idea began to germinate. The hypothesis that civil discourse can take place among FB friends who disagree politically began to form in my mind. How to perform an experimental test of the hypothesis within my own network had not yet developed. I first needed to fully resolve my own grief over Clinton's loss and sublimate it into curiosity. I also needed to learn more about the causes and effects of political polarization.

## Confession of My Own Political Bias; Election Stress Disorder

Before I delve more deeply into the causes and effects of our current unhealthy political polarization and describe the FB experiment I performed, I need to disclose my own political biases and confess to my own nasty political posting. How and why political culture in the US has become so ugly, and the role social media has played in the ugliness, are addressed in the following chapters. What actually happened in the experiment with Facebook is detailed in the final section of the book.

I voted for Obama in each presidential primary and general election in Indiana in which he was a candidate. I felt an affinity for him, because I graduated college from the University of Chicago – he taught at the Law School. And, I lived in Hyde Park (the Obamas' Chicago neighborhood) during college and for a couple years after graduation. When my wife and I lived in Hyde Park was several years before the Obamas moved in. I have never met Barack or Michelle in person. But I am acquainted with Hyde Parkers and U-Chicagoans who know them. These connections gave me a sense of commonality with Obama that I have not shared with any other presidential candidate.

Regardless of the sense of connection, what originally impressed me with Obama was his lonely stand in the US Senate opposing the 2003 invasion of Iraq. This guy, I thought, is one of the few national political-figures with the intelligence to figure out what a disaster invading Iraq will turn out to be, and has the courage to act on his conviction. As President, I thought he performed reasonably well. I appreciated his cautious, pragmatic approach to governing.

I have settled into an appreciation for moderation and pragmatism in politics and governance. A few catch phrases that describe my mature political persuasion are: Fiscal conservative and social liberal; incentivize rather than subsidize; evolution, not revolution; pragmatic problem solving is a better policy than any political ideology; and, human rights tend to improve in a strong economy and human rights tend to help an economy flourish. Barack Obama, I think, would agree with those sentiments.

So, as an Obama supporter in social media, I often "liked" nasty posts about his political opponents and added an "Amen" sort of comment or reply to positive posts about him. I responded to some anti-Obama posts that I could show were factually incorrect by linking to relevant articles or citing actual evidence. I wagged a proverbial finger at friends who circulated false reports about Obama.

The Clinton/Trump contest drew me more deeply into the fray on social media. I actively participate in some anti-Trump threads. And, I made a point of defending Clinton against factually inaccurate posts by friends.

There were clear draw backs to Clinton as a candidate in my mind, but I thought she would largely maintain the pragmatic and slightly left-leaning course Obama had followed. So, I wasn't thrilled to support her, but I thought she was a far better alternative than Donald Trump.

During the primary campaign season, I didn't think Trump was the worst of the Republican candidates, but he was pretty far down my list of preferences. I liked the moderate Kasich.

Many of my conservative friends think that following the left-leaning course of Obama/Clinton is leading the country down a long slide into a socialist-welfare state. Maybe. But Donald Trump as Commander-in-Chief raised the frightening specter in my mind of a narcissic-authoritarian personality with his finger on the button. He did not seem the type to be satisfied just making conservative course-corrections to the leftward drift of the Obama presidency. I imagined him more likely to retard the progress made in the economy, on the environment, and in international relations during the Obama years. I feared he might do real damage to the country and world with his wild promises, lack of interest in facts, and volatile temper.

I did not want to alienate my Trump-supporting friends by attacking their candidate, or them, in Facebook. So, for the most part I stayed out of the fray of the Facebook battles I witnessed. I didn't unfriend anyone for ugly partisan-posting. I rarely gave in to the temptation to fume publicly about noxious statements or actions of Donald Trump on my Facebook page. I did use Twitter to vent and rant during the presidential campaign. The vast majority of my FB posts remained within the bounds of friendly blather.

But, as the tone of the political posts became increasingly mean and hostile as the 2016 election approached my worries about the damage to the body politic from extreme polarization began to mount. Instead of a communications network, Facebook and Twitter had become the front lines of the political firestorm between Clinton and Trump supporters.

While my use of Facebook for political purposes was relatively innocuous compared to many of my FB friends, I, like Donald Trump, regularly used Twitter to vent my feelings about political developments during the 2016 campaign season. I used it as the medium to express my antipathy toward Donald Trump as a candidate. I tweeted snarky comments and silly photos of "the Trumpeter". I compared Trump to Berlusconi and Mussolini with parallel photos attached to my tweets.

In retrospect, those are not my proudest moments in social networking. But I don't think Twitter is a medium that has the potential for much better use. Its inherent limitations make it an inadequate medium for reasoned argument. Clever one-liners and memes, yes; a vehicle to point out a worthy article, indeed. The 140-character limitation is well-designed as a pointer and for verbal fist fights, not developing complex ideas or in-depth discussions. So, I'm less concerned about its contribution to the sickness of the body politic as I am about Facebook's.

As a medium for spleen venting, Twitter's 140-character limit makes it ideal. Better to blast away in a venue designed for flicking right hooks and snapping left jabs than to waste space in Facebook. (Using Twitter as a medium for issuing presidential announcements and conducting diplomacy – that still worries me.) Facebook, on the other hand, has the potential for creating threads of reasoned and literate conversation and argumentation.

Given my political leaning, my evaluation of Trump as a prospective President, and the pundits and polls confident prediction of a Clinton victory, the shock of Trump's election did inspire me to fire off blasts of outrage on Twitter at what seemed to me a terrible decision of the electorate. (It was little consolation that Clinton won the popular vote.) I was not alone. Many Clinton supporters took her loss so hard, "Not my President!" replaced Clinton yard signs. Millions participated in the innocuously named Women's March the day after Trump's inauguration. Speakers at these anti-Trump rallies urged the crowds to resist anticipated Republican reversals of Obama policies.

Trump's surprise win shocked many anti-Trump voters so deeply that a new psychological condition was identified: "Post-Election Stress Disorder".

In just over two short months, the country has experienced polarization, unrest and activism unmatched in recent history. The effects are already evident: A staggering 57 percent of people polled by the American Psychological Association in January said the current political climate is causing them significant stress. Indeed, mental health professionals have coined the terms "election stress disorder" and "headline stress disorder" to describe the plight of many clients.

Michelle Kinder, *Next Avenue*, "3 Ways to Handle 'Post-Election Stress Disorder'," March 6, 2017 (online)

My own initial shock began to wear off within a few weeks after the election. Participating in a discussion group of mostly Clinton supporters at a local Quaker meeting was therapeutic. Grieving together helped heal what felt like an open wound. By the time I joined in the Indianapolis Women's March the day after President Trump's inauguration I had moved through the emotional stages of shock, anger, and sadness into curiosity about what Trump and the Republican Congress would actually do. If they acted contrary to what I thought was in the country's best interest, I could respond appropriately. In the meantime, the healthiest response would be to keep an open mind and see what Trump and the Republican Congress would actually do.

Remaining in a state of shock, rage, or grief would qualify me for a diagnosis of election stress disorder. That was not an attractive option.

There is clear evidence in social media and elsewhere that many Clinton voters are still in a state of rage or grief months after Donald Trump was sworn in as President. Almost three months after the inauguration, I literally ran into a friend on a running trail near my home. I hadn't seen Bob for a couple years. He was standing in the middle of the trail gazing distractedly into the sky. He looked dazed and confused. I asked what was wrong. Bob shook his head and proceeded to tell me he just couldn't get over Trump being elected President.

Instead of enjoying a lovely spring day, Bob was still in mourning over the election of Donald Trump. "I still can't believe it," he said shaking his head slowly from side to side. "I've thought about leaving the country."

A number of my friends offline and online have expressed similar feelings to Bob's. I'm not a politician, physician, or prophet, but blasting away at Trump and his supporters on social media, might give a moment of satisfaction, but it's not an effective psychological remedy or political strategy.

# II. The Case against Siloing and for the Un-Like Minded

*When our fight or flight system is activated, we tend to perceive everything in our environment as a possible threat to our survival. By its very nature, the fight or flight system bypasses our rational mind—where our more well thought out beliefs exist—and moves us into "attack" mode. This state of alert causes us to perceive almost everything in our world as a possible threat to our survival. As such, we tend to see everyone and everything as a possible enemy. Like airport security during a terrorist threat, we are on the look out for every possible danger. We may overreact to the slightest comment. Our fear is exaggerated. Our thinking is distorted. We see everything through the filter of possible danger. We narrow our focus to those things that can harm us. Fear becomes the lens through which we see the world.*

*We can begin to see how it is almost impossible to cultivate positive attitudes and beliefs when we are stuck in survival mode. Our heart is not open. Our rational mind is disengaged. Our consciousness is focused on fear, not love. Making clear choices and recognizing the consequences of those choices is unfeasible. We are focused on short-term survival, not the long-term consequences of our beliefs and choices. When we are overwhelmed with excessive stress, our life becomes a series of short-term emergencies. We lose the ability to relax and enjoy the moment. We live from crisis to crisis, with no relief in sight. Burnout is inevitable. This burnout is what usually provides the motivation to change our lives for the better. We are propelled to step back and look at the big picture of our lives—forcing us to examine our beliefs, our values and our goals.*

The Fight or Flight Response - NeilMD.com
www.thebodysoulconnection.com/EducationCenter/fight.html

**"A house divided against itself cannot stand."**
Abraham Lincoln

Political scientists identified a trend toward greater political polarization in the US prior to President Obama's election. As described in this article published the year Obama was elected:

> Since the 1970s, ideological polarization has increased dramatically among the mass public in the United States... There are now large differences in outlook between Democrats and Republicans, between red state voters and blue state voters, and between religious voters and secular voters. These divisions are not confined to a small minority of activists -- they involve a large segment of the public and the deepest divisions are found among the most interested, informed, and active citizens.
> Alan I Abramowitz and Kyle L. Saunders, *The Journal of Politics*, "Is Polarization a Myth?" 2008

Many of us thought Obama was an inspiring figure as the first African-American (or mixed race) President. Some thought he would be a uniting figure. It didn't turn out that way.

And now, an even more polarizing figure holds the office of President of the United Sates. A Stanford academic opens his online journal article, "Polarization in 2016", with this summary:

> This is the year of Donald Trump. It is the year Republican primary voters applauded proposals to build fences on the border and to ban Muslims. It is the year that the leading Democrat in New Hampshire polls was a self-proclaimed socialist who favored 90 percent top tax rates and a $15 per hour national minimum wage. It is the year we all decided once and for all that those on the other side of the political divide didn't just have different priorities, didn't just hold different opinions, but were out to destroy the country and everything it stands for. Americans in 2016 are more politically divided than ever before.
> Matthew Gentzkow,
> https://web.stanford.edu/gentzkow/research/PolarizationIn2016

A question social scientists have begun to grapple with is whether social media contributes to political polarization or not. Gentzkow's article summarizes the arguments of prominent academics who castigate the

Internet as the Iago-like villain pushing and pulling Americans into hostile camps.

> An early, influential example of this argument is the book Republic.com by Cass Sunstein (2001). Sunstein argues that the Internet is creating "echo chambers," where partisans will hear their own opinions, biases and prejudices endlessly reinforced. He writes: "Our communications market is rapidly moving" toward a situation where "people restrict themselves to their own points of view -- liberals watching and reading mostly or only liberals; moderates, moderates; conservatives, conservatives; Neo-Nazis, Neo-Nazis". This increases polarization and limits the "unplanned, unanticipated encounters [that are] central to democracy itself".
>
> More recently, Pariser (2012) argues that we are not only self-selecting into echo chambers, we are being steered into them whether we like it or not. In trying to show us content we will click on, Google's personalized search results and Facebook's personalized news feeds screen out content we are most likely to disagree with, and create a comfortable bubble of like-minded information.
>
> Epstein and Robertson (2015) argue that the effects on American democracy could be profound. They conduct laboratory experiments in which potential voters are shown manipulated search results that favor one side of the political spectrum or the other. They then ask participants about their voting intentions. They find large effects, which, if extrapolated outside the laboratory, would imply that large companies such as Google could determine the outcome of many national elections.
> (citations omitted)

Yikes! Google could determine the outcome of the next presidential election?!

The Shorenstein Center of the Harvard Kennedy School summarized the findings of a group of studies in an article published May 17, 2015 in *Journalist's Resource* (online), "Does Facebook drive political polarization?" It reported that the Pew Research Center and several university social science departments had shown that "political discussions on Twitter often show 'polarized crowd' characteristics, whereby a liberal and conservative cluster are talking past one another on the same subject, largely relying on different information sources." The research "confirms that groups are disproportionately exposed to like-minded information and that information reaches like-minded users more quickly than users of the opposing ideology. Political talk ... is typically highly partisan and clustered around groups of likeminded users."

And it's getting worse. The Shorenstein Center published its results in May 2015, a year before the polarizing Trump v. Clinton race. My experience on Facebook is consistent with the studies reflecting an increasing polarization along political-ideological lines. As predicted, my friends increasingly posted hostile comments on politically oriented threads and have retreated into like-minded private groups.

The finality of the presidential election results was not an antidote to the irrational passions inflamed by the angry rhetoric of the campaign. Facebook lit up with even greater vehemence after Trump's election and then again at his inauguration. By hurling insults and ridicule at right-wingers my left-wing friends were releasing their fury over Trump's election and taking their revenge for the assaults against Obama my right-wing friends posted during his presidency.

Social media was not serving as a forum of healing with meaningful conversation about where we go from here after the conclusion of the 2016 presidential campaign. It wasn't used as a medium to develop greater understanding between partisans on opposite sides of the political divide. It wasn't even much used as a forum for strategizing on how to respond to the surprising election of a neophyte politician as President whose party would control both Congress and the Senate. Post 2016 election, Facebook was just another place for disappointed Democrats to howl their rage at their political foes; and where Republicans could express their triumphant glee.

Some Trump supporters reveling in their guy's victory aped the outrageous-insulting style he used so effectively in the Republican Primaries. Instead of the stuffy form of address customary in presidential elections, Trump delighted in name-calling. Rather than "my worthy opponent", there was "low energy Jeb", "little Marco", and "lying Ted" in the primaries. He was no more gallant against Mrs. Clinton during the general election campaign. He encouraged his followers with shouts of "Lock her up!" and labeled her "lying Hillary".

Clinton contributed to the below-the-belt style of campaigning Trump started by focusing her campaign on Trump's personal unfitness to be President. She left her comfort zone as a policy wonk to try her hand at negative campaigning. She and her advisors rightly thought Trump was an easy target. But they didn't anticipate that Hillary herself would be as easy a target as she was. The never-ending Congressional and FBI investigations of her emails gave a veneer of credence that she lied and should be locked up.

When the campaign was finally over and the votes counted, instead of swords being lowered, the partisanship of a polarized electorate was mirrored in social media. The hyper-partisanship in Congress was spurred on by post-election heat in social media, and the heat generated in social media encouraged more partisanship among Congressional delegates. Where were the good guys riding in over the horizon to save the country from the spreading disease of extreme polarization?

President Trump was not the gracious winner who would calm the waters and bind up the nation's wounds. After a perfunctory nod to bipartisanship in his inaugural speech, he was back to his habit of madly tweeting away on his smartphone egging his supporters on and throwing rotten eggs at his opponents.

Donald J. Trump✔ @realDonaldTrump Happy New Year to all, including to my many enemies and those who have fought me and lost so badly they just don't know what to do. Love! 8:17 AM - 31 Dec 2016

Donald J. Trump✔ @realDonaldTrump I win an election easily, a great "movement" is verified, and crooked opponents try to belittle our victory with FAKE NEWS. A sorry state! 7:44 AM - 11 Jan 2017

Donald J. Trump✔ @realDonaldTrump The same people who did the phony election polls, and were so wrong, are now doing approval rating polls. They are rigged just like before. 8:11 AM - 17 Jan 2017

The writer and public intellectual Camille Paglia thinks the deepening polarization of the American and European body politics should be diagnosed as suffering from a cultural pathology.

The liberal versus conservative dichotomy, dating from the split between Left and Right following the French Revolution, is hopelessly outmoded for our far more complex era of expansive technology and global politics. A bitter polarization of liberal and conservative has become so extreme and strident in both the Americas and Europe that it sometimes resembles mental illness, severed from the common sense realities of everyday life.
Camille Paglia, *Time*, "Women Aren't Free until Speech Is," March 21, 2017 (online)

Paglia is correct to point out that the deepening polarization of left versus right politics is not limited to the US. Another online *Time* article posted as voting results came in for the May 2017 elections in France described, "The campaign has been unusually bitter, with voters hurling eggs and flour, protesters clashing with police and the candidates insulting each other on national television -- a reflection of the country's deep divisions." Philippe Sotto, "French Cybersecurity Agency to Investigate Emmanuel Macron Election Hacking," May 06, 2017

Rebecca Solnit, in her *Harper's* essay referenced above, argues that politicians and the media are engaged in an unholy alliance of "trafficking in outrage". She's a leftist, but accuses both leftwing and rightwing media outlets and politicians of "making ad hominem attacks, dividing the political world into heroes and villains, giving us this day our daily rage."

So, it's no secret that the US and other democratic republics are ailing with the sickness of extreme polarization. But what to do about it?

Another leftist author-intellectual I admire worried about the animus progressives feel toward Trump voters. In the Winter 2017 issue of *The American Scholar* Amitai Etzioni urged his fellow liberal progressives "who wish for a less reactionary America could begin by trying to understand the Trump voter." "We Must Not Be Enemies" was written a month after Trump was elected and published a month after Trump's inauguration.

> Clearly, not all of these Americans can be reached by new progressive thinking, but respect for their fellow human beings and political prudence suggest that all of them should be approached as if they could be. The question is not only whether a new progressive movement can appeal to the less extreme elements of the Trump constituencies, but also whether progressives can understand the legitimate anger and frustration that many Trump voters felt and still feel, in the hope of creating a more workable, just, and peaceable society.

The way to approach Trump voters is to try to engage them in respectful and rational discourse. Conversely, the way Trump supporters can better understand those on the other side of the political divide is by engaging them in respectful rational discourse. Etzioni isn't urging his fellow progressives to change sides or to alter their own political alignment. He just wants them to treat Trump supporters as adult human beings.

A common insult kids of my generation applied to verbal bullies was: "You can dish it out, but you can't take it." Too many of us have grown up to be that kind of social media bully. We can dish it out, but then block or delete critical replies or unfriend people who offend us. As adults we ought to be able to dish it out and to take it.

Is it really that hard to listen and speak respectfully with people we disagree with politically? The admonition of Etzioni, an internationally respected scholar writing for the journal published by the academic honor society Phi Beta Kappa, is giving his readers the same kind of advice given by Robert Fulghum in the popular book series from the 1990's, *All I Really Need To Know I Learned in Kindergarten.* The implication is that even the best and brightest among us have regressed into angry children misbehaving on the playground.

Indeed, many of us have. It's not from lack of intelligence or education. Learned subscribers of *The American Scholar* need to be reminded of a lesson in civility as do backwoods dwellers in Appalachia, in the inner city, and the suburbs. The refusal to engage in adult conversations across ideological lines is more a problem of maturity, in the sense of tolerance to accept differences, than intelligence or learning.

The response of a FB friend who has advanced degrees from prestigious universities to my invitation to participate in the experimental forum with pro-Trump voters:

> Thank you. Jeff's idea is totally wonderful in theory, but when you factor in racists, bigots, and brain-washed religious fanatics who have not and will not ever listen to facts, reason, and measured attempts to "understand" the fact that they're haters, it won't work. The operative word here is FANATICS. They have abdicated all rights to be treated with respect and courtesy. And the Democrats are only finally opening their eyes to the fact that you can't negotiate with FANATICS. You either fight them on their dirty, ugly, Trumpian turf, or you die.

Current extreme political polarization has not developed without a reason and intention. It is not a historical accident. This may make me seem like a conspiracy freak, but powerful people influencing politics through political action committees (PACs) and the major political parties, along with the ideologically-slanted news media, have decided that it's in their selfish interest to drive an ideological wedge between conservative-leaning and liberal-leaning Americans. These forces oppose moderation and compromise. They benefit from, and encourage, division.

So, it's up to us, the people, to commit ourselves to engage in the kind of respectful conversations Etzioni encourages in order to create better understanding across the political divides. We can't depend on our political leaders and national media to try to bring us together. Too many of the influential class make money and accrue power by inflaming the right/left animus of their consumers and constituents. That's why so many media outlets have become openly partisan. It's why bipartisanship has become a cuss word in Congress. And that's why political campaigns have become so ugly. Inflaming visceral passions and prejudices to divide the country keeps the money pouring into the pockets of the PACs, parties, and politicians.

So, we're going to have to take advantage of our own communication networks to create a better understanding of our political differences. The virtual world of digitized communications has blessed us with numerous ways to do that. At present, Facebook is the best.

What would happen if we declared a suspension of hostilities on our FB pages? Political adversaries could be invited to cross picket lines to engage forthrightly, but respectfully, in discussion threads about political issues with friends on the other side of the political divide. Pragmatic, instead of ideological, solutions to our social, economic, and political problems could be posted and discussed.

While the idea of creating a Facebook forum for open discussion of political topics was forming, questions arose. Is the impulse to attack political rivals so powerful that FB friends would be unable to restrain themselves? The fear of being attacked might be so great friends would prefer not to go out into the open of "no man's land". Wouldn't it be safer to hunker down inside our own trenches in the protective comfort of like-minded allies?

I witnessed an outpouring of mass grief and anger at the post-inaugural Women's March. Resistance was the dominant theme. Offers of reconciliation were not the response from the Trump side. It was mockery and hostility toward the protesters. The Inauguration had no discernible effect in reducing polarization. It was clear that the divide would continue to deepen and widen, not lessen.

I'd had enough. I didn't want to be sucked into unhealthy outrage any longer. So, I decided to try to ward off the disease. My therapeutic discipline would be to try to maintain a conscientious respect for friends who voted differently than me. I would refrain from posting inflammatory or disrespectful remarks about Trump and his supporters on my FB page. I did not want to alienate friends from the community I had developed, even if they were engaging in obnoxious hardcore-partisan posts. (Twitter, on the other hand, would still be an outlet, if I really needed to vent.)

That was the first step I took on Facebook toward developing what became my experiment with civil discourse about political issues. I committed myself to cease my own anti-Trump posting in Facebook. The discipline would allow me to "like" or comment approvingly of critical posts about Trump, but I was determined not to launch a thread which would impugn friends who voted for Trump. (It wasn't easy.)

## *The Spreading Disease of Extreme Polarization*

The disease of toxic political posting continued to spread even after the reality of Donald Trump's presidency was confirmed by his inauguration. The virus was not contained. There were a few weak and despairing calls for bipartisan healing. They went unanswered by the pundits, politicians, press, and furious social media users. The outrage machine was thrumming in high gear, and was not going to power down just because political campaigning ended.

High octane political passion is the new normal. It is with us always whether an election is in the offing or not. Even if you figure out how to duck it on social media, turn on your television or radio and it's there too. Unless you only watch movies, it's become virtually impossible to avoid partisan yapping over the airwaves or through your cable.

I was infected. I am a confessed news junkie. My mother, grandfather, and step-father were journalists who became news editors of the local paper in my hometown. I grew up with it, so that's my excuse for reading, watching, listening, and streaming several hours of news every day. I was being pummeled, not with too much information about hard news, but with the too common editorializing that had steadily crept in to news reporting.

During the campaign season partisan reporting aggravated my fears of a Trump presidency and a kowtowing Congress. I can't control news reporting, but I can control my reaction to it. After the Inauguration, instilling more discipline into how I reacted on social media to the new reality of the Trump presidency would be part of a cleansing.

I wanted to rid myself of the unhealthy anger and grief I'd felt about Trump's election, and I wanted to maintain my network of FB friends that had developed since 2008. Not insulting or ridiculing Trump voters on my own FB page was a step toward regaining a healthier participation in social media. But I wasn't yet ready to advance an agenda beyond that personal discipline.

The idea that became the experiment had not yet fully germinated. I was unaware of any models in social media to try out as a means to fight the spread of the disease. But there was a stirring in my soul to do something.

I consider myself politically independent, and have voted for Republicans and Democrats. My own political journey would be hard to chart. When I was allowed to vote as one of the first cohort of eighteen year-olds granted the vote for the 1972 presidential election, I cast one of the 135 votes in Indiana for Doctor Spock. In law school my politically-connected brother obtained a title for me as the Liaison for College and Young Republicans. I worked as a summer intern for Indianapolis-Mayor Bill Hudnut, a Republican. Before graduating from law school I ran for the Indianapolis City Council in the Democratic Primary.

I have shifted right or left, Republican or Democrat, depending on the candidates and issues. I've voted for independents and third-party candidates. The label that is the most accurate descriptor of my recent politics is independent-pragmatic-moderate.

Not being a political partisan, it grieved me that my FB friends had become more inclined to hurl insults at each other than engage in reasoned and respectful dialogue about political issues. What I witnessed after Clinton's loss and Trump's victory was not winners and losers shaking hands and congratulating each other for a game well played. The nasty tone of the campaign got worse. Feelings ran too high. And feelings, not rational discourse or civil conversation, was what my FB friends wanted to express about Trump.

During the 2016 Presidential primaries I received my first invitation from a FB friend to join a "like minded" group. The invitation described it as "Like-Minded Politically and Socially, a secret group." These groups began popping up with increasing frequency after Trump's victory. The next invitation to such a group described it as "A Place For Progressives/Liberals/Independents To Talk, Secret Group." I was invited to participate in four of these closed groups within two months after Trump's election. This distressed me too.

Not only had friends with different political views ceased engaging in civil discourse, they were now gathering into like-minded collectives, where challenging posts would not be permitted.

When I had given in to the temptation to post angry tweets or FB comments about Trump, it often left me feeling like a young teenager after masturbation – relieved, but a little guilty. When I checked out the private political FB groups, the image of a circle jerk came to mind. Yeah, it might feel good to hoot and bellow your rage against Trump and those who voted for him to an amen-chorus, but is that all there is? How does that group affirmation contribute to your own growth and knowledge?

The fact that Americans are divided along the ideological lines of liberal and conservative, along party lines of Democrat and Republican, and all the other divisions within this diverse country of 325 million, is not a bad or unhealthy thing. It's great that we are such a diverse country. It's challenging, for sure, but it's more interesting to live within a diverse society in which people disagree about politics, economics, religion, and all the other issues these fundamental differences open into. That's why representative democracy with constitutional protections for minorities is the best system for us. There will always be disagreements and polarization around certain issues within a society as richly diverse as the US.

Polarization during a political campaign is an aspect of electoral politics. That's why we have parties. They should represent ideological divisions within the country. Party leaders and candidates will naturally harp on those divisions to some extent, if they think emphasizing party differences will win votes. That sort of competitiveness is a function of a healthy democratic republic.

After the election, the ideal is that the country comes together and the elected politicians from both parties work together to craft laws and policies to benefit all citizens. Partisan competition is to be limited to the campaign seasons of the election cycle. The spectacle of the Presidential Inauguration and swearing in of new Congressional members embodies this ideal. Representatives from both parties, winners and losers, appear together to symbolize the unity of the republic after the election is decided.

But Mitch McConnell's strategy of opposing any Obama initiative so polarized Congress that the 2017 Inauguration and Congressional swearing-in were symbols without substance. McConnell's obstructionist strategy appeared to have worked magnificently. Republicans swept in to power winning a majority of Congressional seats, governorships, and state legislatures before the end of Obama's presidency. Now, they had the White House too. Full-time partisan obstructionism worked.

After the Trump election, many Democrats were convinced they should turn the tables on Republicans. "Not my President!" and "Resist!"

These slogans were shouted at anti-Trump rallies, plastered on signs, and posted in social media. A neighbor even taped a "Not my President!" sign to her trash bin for the neighbors to see every trash-pickup day.

Chuck Schumer and Nancy Pelosi, Democratic leaders in the Senate and House, made it clear they were quite willing to adopt the obstructionist strategy of the Republicans to try to thwart President Trump in rolling back any of the "progressive" gains made during the Obama years. Their revenge was exacted in response to the first two major initiatives of the Trump/Ryan/McConnell regime. Democrats refused to negotiate or compromise on the Republican attempt to repeal and replace the ACA (Obamacare) and the nomination of Judge Neil Gorsuch to the Supreme Court. There were no bipartisan discussions seeking compromises on either of these issues. It was winner take all, a zero-sum game.

That's exactly what the hardcore-grassroots Dems and Repubs expected of their leaders after the Trump victory.

They did it to Obama. So by god, we'll do it to them. Not the New Testament ethic of forgiveness and love your enemy, it is an Old Testament eye for an eye ethic our political leaders are following.

> Much political rhetoric suggests that without anger there is not powerful engagement, that anger is a sort of gasoline that runs the engine of social change. But sometimes gasoline just makes things explode.
> Solnit, *Harper's Magazine*, "Easy Chair", May 2017

However it got started, and whoever is to blame, whatever set it off, the polarization and partisanship have moved beyond what is healthy for a functioning democratic republic. That it had become pathological was evident on my computer screen every time I logged onto Facebook or Twitter after Trump and the Republicans won the 2016 elections.

Some of it was amusing and incredibly creative. There were anti Trump and Clinton tweets which brilliantly expressed their creators' antipathy for the targeted candidates. But most were just crude and vulgar. An example randomly picked: "@WTFisGoingOnDon Everybody is a foreigner SOMEWHERE but Trump is a piece of shit EVERYWHERE". The "celebrity" Scott Baio tweeted an image of Hillary Clinton in front of a sign reading "Cunt", which he labeled "best meme out there".

The meanness being expressed on social media toward politicians and their supporters made Trump's attacks on his opponents look mildly petty. Politicians, PACs, and biased news reporting are not the only guilty parties. Many of us are accessories. And, (to mix a medical with a legal metaphor) social media is a primary means of transmitting the disease.

## *The Case against Siloing*

Siloing: Avoiding dialogue with those of opposing views and only acquiring information and news slanted to your own biased perspective (my definition). The siloing I observed on Facebook during Obama's second term reflected the widening and deepening of the political divide within the US. The Clinton/Trump contest threw it into over-drive.

My progressive-Democrat friend Terri told me she didn't go home for the annual Thanksgiving dinner at her parents' house, because her Tea Party and Trump-supporting sister would be there. With the wounds of the November 8th elections so fresh, Terri could not stand to be in the same room with her sister.

At my family's Thanksgiving gathering, my mother laid down a rule that politics would not be discussed. She knew that my brother and his wife voted for Trump, and my wife and I voted for Clinton. We followed her rule, but less than a month later, my brother emailed me that we should cease communicating after an exchange of angry emails I initiated in reaction to a political blog-post of his.

Political passions have always divided some families, but the Obama presidency and then the unexpected election of Donald Trump have driven many of us to break relations with people on the other side of the political divide. Wakefield Research conducted a survey of 1,000 Americans in April 2017 and found that "24% of Americans in a relationship or married report that since Trump was elected, they and their partner have disagreed or argued about politics more than ever." Jade Scipioni, *Fox Business*, "Married Couples Splitting Over Trump, Study Says", May 08, 2017 (online)

Siloing in the news we consume is increasingly the norm since the creation of talk-radio, then Fox News and the market segmentation along the political spectrum by other cable stations. We like to get news from sources that pander to our own prejudices. Getting news from contrary sources upsets us. Do you know any conservatives who regularly watch MSNBC? Liberals who watch Fox News? Have you heard liberals joke about the idiots and nincompoops who watch Fox? Conservatives who sarcastically refer to MSNBC's fake news? So it follows that we begin to cut ourselves off from acquaintances, friends, and even relatives, who might invade our bell jar of acceptable reality with views that oppose or facts that disrupt.

It is comforting to engage with those who generally agree with us. If you've read articles, watched relevant programs, and used your own experience to reach the conclusion, for example, that human-generated carbon emissions are the major cause of global warming;, then you probably don't think very highly of someone who doesn't believe in climate change. Why would you want to hang out with such a fool? But is she a fool? If you haven't actually explored the issue in conversation, how do you know that she can't offer evidence-based arguments that the human effect on climate change is not the primary cause of global warming?

I'm convinced that carbon emissions and other forms of human pollution of the natural environment are creating negative consequences for the planet and the creatures that inhabit it. I've witnessed the loss of glaciers in the Nepal Himalayas in the 22 years I've regularly visited that area. My experience is consistent with scientific measurements of global warming causing glacier shrinkage, which results in less water for lower lands. Loss of water has a cascading effect on the environment and human communities which is not good.

However, I read a letter to the editor in the Winter 2017 edition of the alumni magazine of the University of Chicago, which gave me pause. The writer disputed the accuracy of the generally accepted methods of measurement of global warming as related to C02 and greenhouse gases in the atmosphere. The author of the letter also disputed environmental scientists' claim that the climate has never had such rapid changes in such a short time. He correlated stream flow and tree ring data from 1580 to the early 1990s to back up his charge that temperature variances in recent years have not been as extraordinary as most earth scientists claim.

The author of the letter is a specialist in "cloud microphysics and computer modeling of atmospheric processes as well as statistical methods". He concluded his letter by quoting Robert Zimmer, President of the University of Chicago: "Having one's assumptions challenged and experiencing the discomfort that sometimes accompanies this process are intrinsic parts of an excellent education."

My understanding of climate change and the human contribution to it has not exactly changed, since reading and thinking about the information in the letter to the *University of Chicago Magazine*. But my comfort in accepting the accuracy of the current conventional wisdom was disrupted. My mind isn't changed on the issue, but I'm more open to considering arguments from the other side. It's a good thing not to be closed minded even about issues that seem to be settled.

If we don't listen to people with views contrary to our own, if we never engage with ideas different from ours, and if our understanding of reality goes unchallenged, how do we learn anything? If we ignore them, we will never understand those who disagree with us let alone ever find any common ground for resolving our differences.

The author and scholar William Deresiewicz claims that the power of "the political correctness police" has become so great on elite private college campuses that students who hold conservative attitudes or traditional beliefs feel compelled to maintain silence about their convictions. In his article, "On Political Correctness" in the Spring 2017 edition of *The American Scholar*, Deresiewicz describes how "the belief system of the liberal elite" has transmogrified into the dominant "religion" on theses campuses. If you are not an adherent to this secular religion, then you are a heretic and will be subject to silencing. One of the other unfortunate effects of the political correctness inquisition is the opposite of being quiet. Some rebels against political-correctness regimes, Deresiewiez notes, are likely to act out with "vituperation" on social media and other venues with displays of racism or bigotry.

Because "the enforcement of dogma makes for ideological consensus," Deresiewiez claims, "Students seldom disagree with one another anymore in class." He is especially peeved at universities that disinvite controversial-extremist (usually rightwing) speakers.

> But the reason to listen to people who disagree with you is not so you can learn to refute them. [I disagree with him on this point, as I think that is a worthy reason to engage with a political opponent.] The reason is that you may be wrong. In fact, you are wrong: about some things and probably about a lot of things. There is zero percent chance that any one of us is 100 percent correct. That, in turn, is why freedom of expression includes the right to hear as well as speak, and why disinviting campus speakers abridges the speech rights of students as well as of the speakers themselves.

Deresiewiez concludes his academic rant in *The American Scholar* with a plea to replace political correctness with rational discourse, which necessarily includes disagreement. "The test of your commitment to free speech as a general principle is whether you are willing to tolerate the speech of others, especially those with whom you most disagree. If you are using your speech to try to silence speech, you are not in favor of free speech. You are only in favor of yourself."

It can be tough to engage with people whose understanding of "the facts" is different than ours. It's more comfortable to have people nod in agreement when out of your mouth issues a brilliant opinion. But, can you remember a seminar class you had in college or class discussions in high school, when fellow students got really worked up about something, like whether Hamlet was indecisive or cunningly decisive? Whether he was nuts, brilliant, or both?

Wasn't it exciting to have those passionate disagreements about an academic issue? Did you ever find your own philosophy or theology challenged in a late night dorm discussion about the meaning of life? In school we challenged our classmates and friends, and they challenged us. Sometimes we persuaded and sometimes we were persuaded. Even if no minds were changed, it was intellectually exhilarating to engage in those debates.

Why have we grown out of that willingness, that joy, to engage in civil and reasoned discussions with other un-like minded adults? Surely being a mature adult does not mean inhabiting an intellectual cocoon in which no one is admitted who would cause me discomfort by arguing a position contrary to my own about climate change or any other topic.

Have we become so weak that we really can't stand to be in a room with Sister Sally because she leans right and we lean left, or vice versa?

A senior partner, Skip Kappes, in the law firm I worked as a young associate lawyer once remarked to me, "The strongest steel is forged in the hottest fire." I was whining about facing a difficult hearing that I was sure I was going to lose. I didn't want to be embarrassed. My elder and mentor knew it would be a growing experience for me to fight a battle I was likely to lose, because it would toughen me intellectually and make me a better lawyer.

If we retire from the intellectual battlefield into silos, we may have the comfort of confirming our own prejudices, but our steel will not become stronger. The highest and best use of our time on this planet is not to be comfortably ignorant of what others think and why they think differently than we do.

### *Love Your Enemies*

A documentary film in the PBS series *Independent Lens*, entitled "Accidental Courtesy", was broadcast on my local station WFYI on February 13, 2017. The film made the case for engaging with people you disagree with as radically as possible. Daryl Davis has spent decades meeting with members of Ku Klux Klan organizations to engage them in conversation. Davis is African-American. The film showed Davis talking to several Klan leaders, including the Maryland Grand Dragon and Imperial Wizard, Roger Kelly. (Davis recounts his experiences in his book, ***Klan-destine Relationships: A Black Man's Odyssey in the Ku Klux Klan.***)

Davis explained his motive: "If enemies are talking – even if they're yelling and pounding the table – they're not fighting." He went on, "It's easy to talk to people you agree with, but what good does that do? You don't change anything just talking to people you agree with."

In the film Davis is criticized by Mark Potok, director of the Southern Poverty Law Center (SPLC), and attacked by Black Lives Matter activists in Baltimore for even speaking with KKK members. The Baltimore activists were radicalized by the death of Freddie Graves in police custody. They considered Davis an "Uncle Tom" and were furious that he would speak with "the enemy". He responded that they were "ignorant" and would remain so, "because they didn't know their enemy."

Potok moderated his criticism of Davis as their conversation lengthened and deepened. He admitted that ultimately they were working for the same objective, harmony, or at least peace, among the races. Potok described what Davis was doing as a "retail" strategy, while the SPLC's strategy is "wholesale" – attacking racism systemically rather than through personal one-to-one relationships.

Daryl Davis's retail strategy is confounding. How can anyone who despises what the Klan stands for, and knows what it is guilty of, engage in civil conversation with Klan leaders?

Davis would be considered very uncool, except that he is an accomplished and very cool musician. He's played professionally in an amazing range of genres from jazz, blues, rock, country, and classic. He played with Chuck Berry, Jerry Lee Lewis, and B. B. King.

Davis reasons that the incredible diversity of the US requires everyone to be open to dialogue with everyone else lest we descend into violent chaos or a race war. His argument for engaging with white-supremacist racists ("those who hate me just because of the color of my skin") is that knowing each other will reduce the chance of irrational hate-based violence.

I spent several years as an advocate-attorney working within the legal system to attack social justice problems, such as fair treatment of renters, consumer protection, jail conditions, and industrial water pollution. So, I've experienced the effectiveness (and the ineffectiveness) of law and government to systematically address social, economic, and environmental issues. But that's not the level at which most of us operate. Few of us are crusading lawyers, idealistic politicians, or a *Mr. Smith Goes to Washington* statesman. The level at which most of us operate in our daily lives is the retail level. So, if we don't engage with people who hold views contrary to our own, we may be sacrificing our only chance to make the world a little better.

If two people develop a more harmonious relationship through a deeper understanding of each other, isn't the world just a little better?

The "Accidental Courtesy" documentary referenced President Obama's speech at the July 2016 memorial service for five Dallas police officers, who were shot ambush-style. The cops were watching over marchers in a peaceful protest against police shootings of black people.

> These things we know to be true. And if we cannot even talk about these things, if we cannot talk honestly and openly, not just in the comfort of our own circles, but with those who look different than us or bring a different perspective, then we will never break this dangerous cycle.

> In the end, it's not about finding policies that work. It's about forging consensus and fighting cynicism and finding the will to make change.

> Can we do this? Can we find the character, as Americans, to open our hearts to each other? Can we see in each other a common humanity and a shared dignity, and recognize how our different experiences have shaped us? And it doesn't make anybody perfectly good or perfectly bad, it just makes us human.

Daryl Davis is engaged in an experiment requiring almost super human courage and tolerance. His life has been threatened by whites and blacks. The idea germinating in my mind was far less radical and far less dangerous. Would Facebook friends with opposing political views willingly engage in conversational threads about divisive political issues? If Davis is

POLARIZED

able to look into the eyes of Klansmen and engage them in civil conversations about race relations, surely Facebook friends with opposing political views could be coaxed into participating in conversational threads about politics.

A social media network, like Facebook, can be transformational at the "retail" level much more efficiently than one-to-one personal meetings. Online networks aren't "wholesale", in Potok's terms. They aren't tools to mandate systemic changes in human relations in the way government and the law can effect change. But, through online networks we can try to change hearts and minds among our own friends and followers. A powerfully attractive message might even go viral and change the way thousands or millions think or feel about an issue or a public figure.

You don't have to secure a location, send notifications of a meeting time and place, or arrange coffee and tea. You can simply post an idea or start a conversational thread. Every person who sees your post might be affected by the message.

Two weeks after I watched "Accidental Courtesy" I launched my experiment on Facebook.


### *Confirmation Bias, Political Gridlock and Obstructionism*

Everybody complains about political gridlock in Washington -- the Democrats, Republicans, the media, your friends over for dinner, the guy sitting next to you at the bar or coffee house. Since everyone is upset about the government not getting things done that it should, why is unyielding partisanship getting worse, not better?

One major factor is ideological siloing.

If the news and information you receive is slanted to conform to your ideological interpretation, then your understanding of the relevant facts to current political issues must be correct. If the people you hang out with to discuss current events and politics tend to agree with each other, then you must be right.

"Confirmation bias, also called confirmatory bias or myside bias, is the tendency to search for, interpret, favor, and recall information in a way that confirms one's preexisting beliefs or hypotheses." *Wikipedia* entry on "confirmation bias".

A consequence of news consumers (including politicians) ideologically or politically filtering the information we are exposed to is the reinforcement of our settled opinions. Information is discounted from sources that report the news differently from our usual ones. If we encounter someone who disagrees with our typical sources, they must be wrong.

Confirmation bias spreads insidiously, because we like how it feels for other people to agree with us. Ideological siloing has qualities similar to drug addiction. We consume news from sources that confirm our biases, because that feels right. We engage with people online that we agree with, because that affirms us. Gathering into collectives of like-minded friends kind of looks to outsiders like addicts hanging out in a crack house.

The obvious way to overcome confirmation bias is to engage with credible sources of information which challenge our biases. A one-time encounter won't do it. Being confronted with credible facts which contradict our ideology actually tends to cause a "backfire effect".

> ... research shows that when presented with accurate information that contradicts their current political perspective, people tend to invest more strongly into their current political beliefs instead of changing their mind, a thinking error known as the backfire effect.
> Gleb Tsipursky, *Scientific American*, "Sometimes, Facts Can Actually Trump Ideology," May 19, 2017

Tsipursky's research involved using behavioral science techniques with talk radio hosts. He found that hardcore ideologically-conservative hosts did change their positions on specific issues when they received information from several sources they considered credible in the course of extended conversations. Their ideology didn't change, but their minds were changed from positions they instinctively took on particular political issues. The key was engaging them in extended conversations, which helped the radio hosts to absorb information which they initially rejected on ideological grounds.

Being challenged can be painful. When you push yourself harder in the gym than your usual workout, it hurts. When your opinions and beliefs are challenged in conversation, it can be difficult to take. It's hard on your ego to lose an argument. Just being confronted with information that conflicts with our settled opinions is difficult. The typical reaction is to dig in and resist ideas and information that conflicts with our beliefs and opinions.

Your forehead is getting hot and the volume of your voice is rising. You know that feeling. The discomfort of engaging in heated debate registers at a basic physiological level. Better just to avoid that kind of stress.

But a muscle that is not stressed does not get stronger.

Avoiding alternative sources of information and huddling with the like-minded fosters a political climate of winner takes all. When people on different sides of political (or any) issues receive distinctly different reports and interpretations about current events and relevant facts, the other side's position is incomprehensible. When you can't even agree on what the facts are – because yours are from MSNBC and hers are from Fox – how can you possibly find any common ground? The other side is not being realistic!

When we do not engage in respectful conversation with people whose views are different from our own, we are unable to find common ground for any compromise. Those disagreeable fools are stupid and intransigent. They are blind to the way things really are.

Ideological siloing makes politics a zero-sum game. When bipartisan compromise is out of the question, then governance and legislation require a power bloc strong enough to impose its will. Any solution to a difficult problem, which would respect the legitimate concerns of those out of power, becomes unattainable. If no party or caucus has enough votes to push its agenda through, gridlock ensues.

Republicans became the majority party in 2010, midway through President Obama's first term. Mitch McConnell issued his order of noncooperation with the President. Political "gridlock" entered the popular parlance.

Obama failed to persuade any Republican senators in 2009 to vote for the Affordable Care Act (Obamacare). But other legislation progressed through the Congress with the traditional jawboning by the President and compromises between party leaders. Most significantly, a series of bills to stimulate economic recovery from the Great Recession of 2008-09 passed with bipartisan support.

After McConnell and the Republicans developed their obstructionist strategy in 2010, immigration reform, how to resolve the fate of prisoners in Gitmo, further economic stimulus initiatives and tax reforms, all were stymied by gridlock. Congressional Republicans even briefly shut down the federal government in 2013 rather than negotiate compromises in the federal budget with the Democrats.

After the 2016 election of Trump, partisan Democrats were beating the drum for retaliation. Calls for "total resistance" by grassroots organizations put pressure on Congressional Democrats to repay Republicans for McConnell's obstructionist strategy. They demanded an eye for an eye.

The first big test was President Trump's nomination of Neil Gorsuch to fill Justice Scalia's seat on the Supreme Court. Since the Repubs blocked President Obama's nomination of Merrick Garland by refusing to hold hearings, the Dems planned to filibuster the vote on Gorsuch. The issue was settled by the Repubs choosing "the nuclear option". They changed the rule requiring 60 votes for confirmation of judicial nominations by a President. Gorsuch was approved on an almost-straight party-line vote (three Democratic senators did vote "yes").

In this political climate, every controversial issue is winner-take-all. As undemocratic as the 60-vote rule seems on the surface, the reason for requiring 60 votes to confirm judicial nominees was to force compromises. If a President nominated a judge that was so extreme or unqualified that the nominee could not attract votes from the other party, then that judicial nominee was probably inappropriate. The rule was intended to encourage Presidents to nominate qualified and moderate jurists. Extremists and unqualified nominees might get "Borked".

"Borked" was coined as a term after President Reagan's nomination to the Supreme Court, Robert Bork, was blocked by Senate Dems after a savage grilling during his confirmation hearings. The current Dems planned the same fate for Trump's nomination of Gorsuch, even though Gorsuch is well-qualified and probably less extreme than Scalia. The Dems were retaliating for McConnell's refusal to give Obama's nominee, Merrick Garland, a hearing. But the Repubs torpedoed the Dems' plan with the nuclear option. Out with the 60-vote rule, and in with Judge Gorsuch.

Hyper-partisanship requires members of the party with a majority to stick together for the party to pass its legislative agenda. The dominant party can't count on moderates in the other party to ally with them for bipartisan compromises.

So, ideological differences within the Republican Party doomed the initial Trump/Ryan American Health Care Act of 2017. The Freedom Caucus within the Republican Party held fast to its demand for a market-based healthcare system. The Congressional Dems refused to provide any support. Paul Ryan ran around like a chicken with its head cut off trying to cobble together a compromised version of the bill that would pass. He failed.

Only moderate Republicans within the House were willing to engage in actual give and take over healthcare reform. The Freedom Caucus wouldn't budge and the Dems wouldn't budge. There weren't enough moderate Republicans to pass the bill. So, the Republican promise to repeal and replace Obamacare failed.

In the current political climate bipartisan compromise is considered treasonous to the base. Pragmatic compromises, which recognize a diversity of legitimate interests, modeled by (maybe mythologized about) Ronald Reagan and Tip O'Neill, is a historical relic. Federal legislating will remain a zero-sum game, unless and until respect and goodwill are restored within the US political system.

Respect and goodwill for political opponents may have to start at the grassroots level to spur our political leadership in that direction. Extreme partisanship is being pushed upward from voters as hard as it is being pushed downward by PACs, political parties, and politicians. If a movement toward moderation is not going to come from the top, what better way to start it than promoting civil discourse on our own Facebook pages?

# III. Can Facebook Resuscitate Our Dying Body Politic?

*The state of the kingdom, then, is like a human body and so Aristotle will have it in Book V of the Politics. As, therefore, the body is disordered when the humors flow too freely into one member of it, so that member is often thus inflamed and overgrown while the others are withered and shrunken and the body's due proportions are destroyed and its life shortened; so also is a commonwealth or a kingdom when riches are unduly attracted to it.*
      Oresme, "De moneta", a commentary on Aristotle's **Politics**, 1356

## *Why Facebook?*

Mark Zuckerberg posted in Facebook on August 27, 2015: "We just passed an important milestone. For the first time ever, one billion people used Facebook in a single day. On Monday, 1 in 7 people on Earth used Facebook to connect with their friends and family." On February 26, 2017 *The Telegraph* posted an online article by Lauren Davis claiming that, "82% of the world's population, excluding China, have a Facebook account and four in 10 people use the platform regularly." Facebook has been and "remains the largest online community," according to the Davis article ("Is your daily social media usage higher than average?").

Futurists predict an even more intimately connected virtual world.

Five billion human minds are therefore about to come online, mostly via sub-$50 smartphones. And unlike the two billion who preceded them, their first experience of the Internet may not be clunky text, but high-resolution video and a fast connection to whatever grabs their imagination. This is a social experiment without historical precedent...

It's certainly possible to imagine a beautiful scenario in which: For the first time in history every human can have free access to the world's greatest teachers in their own language; people discover the tools and ideas to escape poverty and bigotry; growing transparency forces better behavior from governments and corporations; the world starts to gain the benefit of billions of new minds able to contribute to our shared future; global interconnection begins to trump tribal thinking.

But for that to have even a chance of happening, we need to get ready to engage in the mother of all attention wars. Every global company, every government and every ideology has skin in this game. It could play out in many different ways, some of them ugly. Christopher J. Anderson, *Edge*, "The Breathtaking Future of a Connected World," May 8, 2017 (online)

Facebook offers the largest platform in the history of human communications for a "regular citizen" to be heard and to try to influence others. And Facebook, despite the current cultural tendency toward polarization and siloing, has the greatest potential of creating positive civil-engagement among people with clashing perspectives than any other medium of communication. Facebook users can get on board to be part of "the beautiful scenario ... of new minds able to contribute to our shared future ... to trump tribal thinking." Or, we can join the forces that will try to make the future of interconnected minds "ugly".

In 2010, at the behest of Facebook, a team of social scientists began studying the diversity, or lack thereof, in sharing information among Facebook users. In 2012 results of the initial studies were posted on the Facebook page of Eytan Bakshy as an article, "Rethinking Information Diversity in Networks," January 17, 2012. Bakshy's team eventually compiled statistics on 10.1 million FB users in their study of sharing news content on Facebook. His group concluded that, "there is significant viewing of 'cross cutting news content'." Eytan Bakshy, "Exposure to Ideologically Diverse News and Opinion on Facebook," *Science*, May 7, 2015.

According to Bakshy's findings, many Facebook users were receiving and sharing information which did not confirm their own biased views. That's what is meant by "viewing cross cutting news content". However:

> Sharing is not symmetric, with liberals showing less diversity, ideologically speaking, in friendships. Despite the slightly higher volume of conservatively aligned articles shared, liberals tend to be connected to fewer friends who share information from the other side, compared to their conservative counterparts. 24% of the hard content shared by liberals' friends are cross-cutting, compared to 35% for conservatives.
> (The Shorenstein Center's summary of Bakshy's Facebook research)

These statistics might surprise liberals who like to think of themselves as more tolerant than conservatives. But the relevant point here is that almost one-quarter of information liberals were sharing was of a conservative slant, and just over one-third of the news content conservative FB users were sharing had a liberal slant. Of course, this also means that in 2010-11 two-thirds to three-quarters of the information FB users received and shared confirmed their own ideological biases.

Other statistics developed by Bakshy's group could be seen as even more encouraging: "How much cross-cutting content individuals encounter depends on who their friends are and what information those friends share. If individuals acquired information from random others, approximately 45% of the hard content liberals would be exposed to would be cross cutting, compared to 40% for conservatives." Because more information posted was conservatively slanted, according to Bakshy, liberals would necessarily encounter more conservatively-aligned information.

Still, even if 40-45% of the "hard content" information FB users randomly received in 2010-11 was from an ideological perspective different than their own, that means that a majority of the information they received was consistent with their ideological predilection.

Now, keep in mind that Bakshy's team performed their research during Obama's first term. The conclusion that there was significant sharing of cross-cutting content does not contradict my experience on Facebook during that period. It was after Obama's victory over Romney in 2012 that I began to notice the increasing incidence of mean-spirited posting in Facebook and Twitter, which began to drive users into hostile camps. And, it was after the Trump defeat of Clinton in 2016 that I received multiple invitations to join like-minded private groups.

The extreme polarization in the culture and in social media that social scientists have identified as a civic problem began after the conclusion of the Bakshy studies of Facebook use. So, it's no surprise that his research presents a more rainbow picture of FB use.

The Pew Research Center asserts, "A majority of Americans now say they get news via social media, and half of the public has turned to these sites to learn about the 2016 presidential election." *Pew Research Center*, "Social Media Update 2016: Facebook usage and engagement is on the rise, while adoption of other platforms holds steady," November 11, 2016 (online)

The statistics may be confusing or enlightening, but the long and short of it is that millions of Americans are learning through social media what's going on in the world. Or, they think they are learning, but many are only getting a slanted picture of reality which confirms their own biases.

Prior to 2012 Facebook was a more tolerant and open environment than it is now. Bakshy's studies do show that Facebook has been, and so, can be, a medium for significant exchange between users with different political perspectives. That's a hopeful sign, but looking to the past for hope can be dangerously misleading.

The more common experience since the 2016 political campaigns began is that people are choosing to hunker down in social/political silos. A loop has developed in which the polarization of politics is influencing social media users, and the polarization of social media users influences voter patterns. Polarization in social media increases polarization in politics, and vice versa.

Instead of trying to ameliorate unhealthy polarization, the current powers that be within social media may be intentionally aggravating it. According to an article in *Slate*, Twitter has changed what users see when they open their feed from a chronology of tweets to the most popular tweets based on an algorithm. The consequence is that the popular tweeters within your feed will be the ones whose tweets most likely go viral. Those with the largest platforms already have the furthest reach. Their voices will be amplified even greater, while contrary views will get even less attention.

But you can't see more of some kinds of tweets without seeing less of others, and the hidden consequences of that equation could affect us all. As it gradually tightens the loops in Twitter's social fabric, the algorithm risks further insulating its users from people whose viewpoints run counter to their own -- a phenomenon, already rampant on Facebook, that has contributed to the polarization of the American electorate and the Balkanization of its media.

Facebook has taken the brunt of the blame for the fake news and sensationalism that polluted political news in the 2016 U.S. presidential election, both because it is bigger and because its more potent algorithm lends itself to those pitfalls. But Twitter played a role, too, and with the world's most powerful person setting national policy via tweets on a daily basis, the service has never been more influential than it is today.

Will Oremus, *Slate*, "Twitter's New Order Inside the changes that could save its business -- and reshape civil discourse," March 5, 2017

As noted, Facebook was harshly criticized for the spread of fake news during the 2016 presidential campaign. It responded by creating a system intended to limit, if not eliminate, fake news. As described by the BBC:

Facebook, which came under heavy criticism for allowing fake news to be circulated during the election period, has taken steps to combat the issue.

One of those steps is the enlisting of the International Fact Checking Network (IFCN), a branch of the Florida-based journalism think tank Poynter. Facebook users in the US and Germany can now flag articles they think are deliberately false, these will then go to third-party fact checkers signed up with the IFCN.

Those fact checkers come from media organizations like the Washington Post and websites such as the urban legend debunking site Snopes.com.

The third-party fact checkers, says IFCN director Alexios Mantzarlis "look at the stories that users have flagged as fake and if they fact check them and tag them as false, these stories then get a disputed tag that stays with them across the social network."

Another warning appears if users try to share the story, although Facebook doesn't prevent such sharing or delete the fake news story. The "fake" tag will however negatively impact the story's score in Facebook's algorithm, meaning that fewer people will see it pop up in their news feeds.

Mike Wendling, **BBC Trending**, "Solutions that can stop fake news spreading," 30 January 2017 (online)

However, IFCN director Mantzarlis is quoted later in the same article expressing doubt about the ultimate effectiveness the new system will be in combating the spread of fake news.

Mantzarlis says there is as of yet no firm evidence that this actually stops fake news spreading on a large scale, and there are questions over how sustainable the program might be. Facebook is not paying the IFCN members to provide fact-checking services. There's also nothing stopping the fake news from being posted and spread in the first place -- and perhaps quite widely before being tagged.

"There is a lag, so until and unless a story is flagged as false that story does continue to spread on the social network," says Mantzarlis.

Facebook's new system of flagging fake news has even been criticized for creating opportunities to game the system by those who want to suppress sharing from certain perspectives and of certain ideologies. It might boomerang and limit debate among ideological adversaries instead of encouraging dialogue among those with different points of view.

All systems can be gamed, but in the case of Facebook, we've already seen a steady stream of important groups and pages shut down -- likely prompted by "community" reporting of those pages. While in theory this may seem a viable approach, in practice reporting is often used as a tactic by those who disagree with a certain view or ideology.

Most prominently this has been seen with Syrian opposition groups using Facebook to document and report on the ongoing civil war. Facebook does not disclose information about who reported whom, making it impossible to confirm these theories. But the pro-Assad Syrian Electronic Army (SEA) has publicly gloated about this tactic. "We continue our reporting attacks," read a typical post from December 9 on the SEA's Facebook page.

It's thus easy to envision activist groups flagging 'false' news stories en masse based not on their factual content, but on their desire to silence an opposing or dissenting voice. Once a flagged news story has disappeared from our feeds it's unclear if there's a way to challenge the 'false' assignment, or even a way to see a list of the stories that have been blocked.
Tom Trewinnard, ***First Draft News***, "How to stop fake news on Facebook," June 16, 2015 (online)

If the management of Twitter is encouraging siloing and Facebook's attempts at limiting the viral spread of false information is a dud, what's to be done? It's up to us users of social media to take responsibility ourselves. At least within our own community of friends and followers we can take a stand for open, respectful, and rational discourse. We can combat fake news by posting factual reports from neutral/objective sources. Snopes.com is a fact-checking resource everyone concerned with correcting false reports should be familiar with and use.

The spread of polarization, siloing, and false reporting should concern every citizen no matter what your political affiliation. These are not healthy developments in our politics or society. I am cynical enough about our political system and modest enough about my limited influence as a citizen-voter not to expect to have any significant impact on party politics or government. But I do think the viral capacity of social media, particularly Facebook, has the potential to create a ripple of change spreading out through social networks. My experiment with rational discourse on Facebook could influence others to try it. It might serve as a model for others to encourage conversations among social media users of different political, social, or religious persuasions. As President Trump says, "What the hell do you have to lose?"

With its 1.86 billion monthly active users Facebook is the largest "community" of connected communicators in human history. Facebook dwarfs all other social media in user numbers. 79% of American adults use Facebook as their primary online medium, according to the Pew Research Center. Instagram ranks second at 32%. Within this massive universe of interconnectedness, my voice is surely not a lone voice crying in the wilderness. There must be many others who can imagine Facebook as a place where civil discourse among friends with a wide range of political views can occur.

The experiment that took shape in my mind five weeks after the Trump inauguration was simple enough. It would begin by posting a question to FB friends asking whether they were willing to engage in reasoned and respectful debate about current political issues.

Would anyone agree to participate? If they did, would it degenerate into a rancorous exchange of insults between pro and anti Trump friends? The only way to find out was to ask the question.

### *Don't Turn the Other Cheek*

I have given in to the temptation of intolerance in my social media networks. I blocked a Twitter follower, whose criticism of one of my books stung my authorial pride. I came close to doing the same thing on Goodreads, but was restrained by my thicker-skinned wife. No one should accept insults or ad hominem attacks on social media or in any venue or medium. But we should have enough backbone not to hide from opposing opinions and reasoned criticism, even when we disagree with the other's version of the facts, analysis, or conclusions. Rather than turn the other cheek, it would be more productive to engage the adversary.

Easier said than done.

Social media is a venue which allows users to attack and insult from a distance. You can troll using a fake ID. Users can hide from challenges and confrontations by huddling in closed/private like-minded groups. This ability to attack impersonally has created a way to shelter users from responsibility for what they "say" to others. The distancing of digital communication has lowered the bar for taking responsibility for what we say to others.

So there are inherent impediments, due to the nature of social media, to developing a welcoming forum for civil discussions about divisive issues. Still, the premise I was determined to test was that everyone who participates in a conversation thread about controversial political issues would benefit by engaging in direct exchanges with friends who have different takes on the issues. A few friends, maybe many, would see no benefit in consorting with the enemy. But surely some of my 680 FB friends would think it was worthwhile to learn what their political "opponents" thought and why. It would be valuable, if for no other reason, than to be better armed in the next political struggle by understanding the "enemy". (Sun Tzu warns in *The Art of War* that to defeat your enemy you must know him.) Better yet, participants might actually find common ground and room for compromise on divisive issues.

Even if no minds were changed through the discussion threads, gaining a better understanding of different points of view should be interesting and educational. It would offer a personal growth experience, and it might create more meaningful connections among the participants.

I didn't expect pro and anti Trump FB friends to join in a Kumbaya sing-along. I did think it possible that some common values would be discovered and common ground found, despite political and ideological differences.

A fundamental challenge of human civilization is to find ways for neighbors to live peacefully and cooperatively in communities. Allowing the stronger willed or better armed to walk over the rest of us is not the best solution. Domination of the many by one or a few is undemocratic and contrary to American civic values. As a political society we don't "turn the other cheek" to those who try to manipulate or coerce us. Giving in to those who shriek the loudest has not been and should not be the American way.

One of the reasons the USA became a global super power is that our culture and educational system has encouraged open inquiry in the sciences and diverse expression in the arts. An educated, confident, and diverse population should have lively political debates. Elections should be hotly contested. A free and open society will have a wide spectrum of perspectives and opinions.

Who would want to discourage healthy debate and argument about political, social, and economic issues? Close-minded ideologues, religious fanatics, and those who profit by manipulating voters, that's who. I assumed that some of my FB friends are, indeed, too close-minded even to consider engaging in conversation with political opponents. And some might be so brainwashed by political con artists that their participation would be zombie-like – mouthing the platitudes that reflect the biases that are daily confirmed within their information silos.

What I hoped for was respectful and rational debates in threads I could start by posing questions about "hot" political issues. It would be interesting to learn who would be willing to try. What are the political leanings of those that would participate? Would pro and anti Trump friends of mine, who are unacquainted with each other, rise above the fury the presidential campaign generated to engage in rational evidence-based argument? Or, were tempers still so frayed that they would just resort to name-calling?

## *Tolerant and Respectful Competition*

Without tolerance and respect for political and ideological differences, the people on the losing side of an election or a legislative issue will feel like defeated losers in a rigged system. It's much easier to accept an adverse decision when you've been heard and treated with respect. When opponents in a political dispute actually try to understand why they differ, there is a possibility of compromise. It's difficult to negotiate compromises with people you think are out of touch with reality. They will seem stupid or ignorant of the way things really are.

It is a challenge to respect the other side in an adversarial system, like we have in the US. Good sportsmanship requires that, but good sportsmanship has been out of vogue since Vince Lombardi's oft quoted, "Winning isn't everything, it's the only thing." In America we love competition, and we love to win.

Our economic system is competitive and our legal and political systems are designed to be adversarially competitive. Opposing parties are represented in court, and opposing parties have representatives in government. The political competition even spills over into the news media. Newspapers are known to be Republican or Democratic on their editorial pages. Cable news networks and radio stations also tend to favor one party over the other in their news commentary. News reporting is theoretically objective, but how objective it is may depend on how fierce is the news network's loyalty to a political party.

Adversarial competitiveness as a fundamental aspect of American culture reflects a reality about our people. The citizens of the US may be the most culturally and demographically diverse population in the history of nations. So, of course, we have disagreement and different opinions and interests on most issues. Our news media has become so obsessed with analyzing issues in terms of how different "identity groups" are affected to the point that it's difficult to discern any unity in our diversity. One might wonder what's become of the unum in e pluribus unum.

Americans tend to feel a sense of unity and national purpose at the beginning of a war, especially if the homeland is attacked ala' Pearl Harbor and 9/11. Otherwise, our cultural and ethnic diversity syncs up nicely with our love of competition. Let economic and political competition decide who is on top and who is on the bottom.

Unlike monolithic and traditional cultures, Americans are so diverse even generalizing about our love of competition is misleading. Many citizens think the fascination with competitive sport is childish and even brutish. Easter philosophy is attractive to a fair number of us, in part, because it de-emphasizes a competitive approach to life. Our tradition-bound legal system has transformed itself in recent decades to encourage mediation rather than litigation.

In the US we don't even have a uniform set of culturally accepted ethical principles. For example, on the fundamental ethical scale of selfish/unselfish, some of us primarily value selfish material-interests. Others highly value sacrificial service. Most of us land somewhere on the spectrum between the extreme poles of completely selfish and utterly unselfish. Our system of regulated capitalism reflects this balance. We want freedom to produce and consume, but we also want an economy which uplifts and doesn't exploit the weak and unwary. Only doctrinaire capitalists and socialists would tip the scale to one extreme or the other. But the arguments over what is the proper balance began before the 13 Colonies won their freedom from the English Crown and continue to this day.

Consumers and producers in a dynamic economy have the freedom to express different values and preferences. Similarly, in a democratic republic citizens will disagree about all manner of political preferences. What is the just and fair amount of taxes? How much of our money does the government really need? There will never be uniform agreement on how much we should be taxed and how best to allocate taxes and national resources. What percentage of the budget should be spent on domestic programs versus defense? Which is more important, freedom of travel and welcoming immigrants or secure borders? Is abortion a right or is it murder? Voters, candidates, and political parties will line up differently on every major issue.

We are not a monolithic society, and we tend to value innovation over tradition. America is dynamic and litigious about our individual rights. We have many disagreements about what is and isn't in the national interest. Our American political apparatus, like our economy, is designed to incorporate a diversity of interests and preferences. The underlying assumption of both systems is that competition will drive us forward to find the best solution out of the many possible ones. Producers compete to develop and sell the most attractive products. Political parties compete to nominate the most attractive and popular candidates. Candidates compete to convince voters that they are better leaders than their opponents.

Consumers are usually, but not always, satisfied with the products they purchase. Voters are usually satisfied with the candidates they voted for. That's why there is consumer brand loyalty and why incumbents usually get reelected. Unfortunately, history proves that consumers and voters do not always make the best choices. Our economic and political systems are human, so they are imperfect.

Although many Americans idealize competition, winning really isn't everything or the only thing. In politics, it's actually governing which is the true test of success. Winning an election is just making it through the interview and hiring process. The actual job starts after the election is won.

In the last election the political competition descended into a contest of name-calling, attack ads, fake news stories, and attempted manipulation by Russian hackers. The dueling campaigns tried to touch voters at the visceral level to tap into their outrage, rather than engage us with civil debate about qualifications and policy. The unfortunate effect was to push voters toward the slanted sources of information that confirmed our biases rather than enlightened us with fresh ideas. The campaigns got so ugly and bitter, no wonder we wanted to escape from it into private groups of like-minded friends.

But voters have a responsibility to resist being duped by fake news, seduced by outrage-producing attack ads, and talking politics only with the like-minded. Otherwise, our political participation is no better than the purchase habits of uninformed consumers.

There are consumers who are satisfied with a brand, and will never consider another. They are uninformed, because they have not done comparison shopping. The citizen who always votes party-line and avoids news sources that challenge his conventional understanding is an uninformed voter.

Uninformed consumers are more likely to buy shoddy products and pay more for them than the informed consumer. Uninformed citizens are more likely to vote for candidates that do not serve the best interests of that self-same voter or the country.

After Trump's victory I saw posts in social media to the effect that his election should not be accepted. After his inauguration I saw signs at the

Women's March to the effect that Trump's presidency is illegitimate. It's one thing to demand resistance of your Congressional representative to the Trump and Republican agenda. It's another to mean it when you say, "not my President".

As Barack Obama famously said after his 2008 victory, "Elections have consequences." Those who only accept results when their side wins and bawl in rage like frustrated babies when their side loses should question their own political maturity and democratic values.

Democracy means that someone you may think is a misogynist, a fool, and dangerous is your President, if he wins the election. Even if he only wins the electoral vote and loses the popular vote, he's still your President. Whine and bitch, if that's how you want to spend your time; it doesn't change who occupies the White House. Now, if you are out working hard to win the 2018 Congressional elections, working for a candidate to challenge Trump in the next presidential election, or encouraging your Congressional rep to sponsor a bill of impeachment, that's not *just* whining.

A *Huffington Post* article in "Weekend Roundup" compared the way the Chinese Communist Party chooses its leaders to the multi-party democratic process in the Netherlands. The Chinese Communist Party Congress and Dutch elections occurred the same week in March 2017. The essential difference, according to the author, is that the Chinese Communist Party operates by "consensus building" while Western democracies engage in competitive elections. The rough and tumble politics of representative democracies have the advantage of giving every citizen a vote, but there is a disadvantage.

> Within this strength of diverse participation lies its flaw: the growing inability to forge a governing consensus out of the exploding cacophony of voices and interests. And, as we've seen in the United States on policies ranging from Obamacare to climate change, when all-out competitive partisanship destroys consensus among the body politic, the democratic transfer of power can mean a complete rupture from policies endorsed by most voters only four years earlier. Nathan Gardels, *Huff Post*, "Weekend roundup: As the West fragments, China cements a path ahead," March 18, 2017

That is a risk with democracy. But the risk is supposed to be reduced by voters and the elected representatives ending the competition when the election results are finalized. After that, winners and losers are supposed to work together for the good of the country. Not agreeing with each other in all instances, but being mature enough to engage in adult conversations and compromises aimed at solving the country's problems.

My first year in law school we were taught that, for the legal system to find truth and do justice, all parties and interests must be represented in the process. It doesn't work if only one side is heard. Opposing counsels are required to be respectful of each other, and each one is allowed a fair opportunity to present their side of the case. A legal proceeding conducted properly is both a presentation of evidence and a debate about what the evidence proves. Emotional appeals are allowed. The system is human, not a computer algorithm. Mistakes will be made. But sheer emotion will generally not persuade a judge or jury to ignore the weight of the evidence. A political campaign has a similar dynamic with the voters sitting as the judge and jury.

In a jury trial each side presents its version of the relevant facts. In closing arguments the attorneys interpret the evidence for the jury and ask jurors to follow the logic of their argument to reach a favorable judgment. The lawyers are competing to convince the jury that their argued-for-result is the best one, the most just and true one. It's not perfect, and the result is not always correct. But it's pretty damn good in comparison to most of the alternatives. The same goes for our political system when functioning properly.

Informed voters listen to both sides and weigh the evidence to decide which lever to pull. In a trial the jury has to listen to both sides. They can't escape the courtroom while the trial is in session. An armed bailiff will escort you to the restroom, if you need a pee break. But that same armed bailiff will bar your escape, if you try to make a run for the door. Like it or not, jurors will see the evidence and hear the arguments of the lawyers.

Voters are not forced to pay attention or to use their reasoning powers to reach conclusions about who is the best candidate and which party has the best platform. It's up to us voters to make the effort to listen to both sides and use our powers of reason to make our best judgments on candidates. If we don't do that, we betray our duty as citizens to fully participate in the secular-sacred act of democratic citizenship.

For the political system to work most effectively, citizens must be informed consumers of political products. Casting our votes in elections is as important as jurors voting on a verdict. Voters need to sift through the evidence and weigh the arguments of each candidate and party. Jurors talk to each other during deliberations. They argue among themselves about the evidence and which side has made the strongest case. Citizens ought to be talking to, and arguing with, each other before deliberately casting our votes.

These discussions ought to be year round, not just before and after elections. We are the employers of the candidates who won their jobs to govern. Like good personnel managers, we need to watch over our chosen representatives and regularly evaluate their performance.

We can do that in person, but we can also take advantage of the biggest interpersonal communications network ever developed – Facebook -- to engage with people across the whole political spectrum. If we maintain that level of engagement, and do it civilly and respectfully, it won't feel like a devastating loss if our preferred candidate loses. We will understand, through dialogue with them, why the other side liked their candidate better than ours. If we win, we will understand why some voters disagreed with us, and we will not hold them in contempt for their ignorance and stupidity.

Minds may not be changed through engagement with political opponents, but understanding will increase. That would sow the seeds for making reasonable and pragmatic bipartisan compromises, which will be supported by voters. If we behave like good sports in our political competitions, we are likely to be able to shake hands, win or lose, and get on with working together to solve the problems that need to be addressed.

Why not give it a try? We have nothing to lose but some of our "friends". If we don't try to promote civil discussions about important issues, then we leave the field to dogmatic ideologues, attack artists, and trolls.

### *Politics as an Existential Contest*

It's a fair question to ask whether the polarization that's developed between supporters/opponents of Obama and now Trump is historically greater than normal. Is it really worse now than ever? Americans always get worked up during presidential elections, and some level of residual animosity remains after the campaign ends. Are we really more divided now than in the past, or is the media just making it seem that way?

George W. Bush eked out two electoral wins, the first one over Al Gore by the vote of one Supreme Court Justice, Sandra Day O'Conner. She cast the fifth vote for a five to four decision in favor of Bush. Like Trump, 'W' lost the popular vote. He needed the Florida electoral votes to be declared the winner. The Supreme Court had to make the final decision on who won the election, because the vote in Florida was so close and messed up with "hanging chads" and other problems it had to be litigated. Many Democrats are still furious about it and think Gore got screwed.

Bush's Gallup Poll of Approval Rating dipped as low as 25% the last year of his two-term presidency. Obama's approval rating sank as low as 37% during his second term. At the end of the second month of the Trump presidency his approval rating by Gallup hit a historic low of 40% for a new US President. Newly elected Presidents usually retain the approval of their supporters early in their first term, so it's very unusual for the rating to dip below 50% just after the inauguration. But still, that's above the lowest approval rating during the terms of Trump's immediate two predecessors. The disapproval of Trump may, in part, be explained as the same buyers' remorse many Americans had about the two Presidents preceding Trump. Maybe we've just become fickle and impatient in how we feel about our Presidents. Or, were we particularly feckless in our recent choices?

Ronald Reagan's approval rating remained well above 60% for most of his eight years in office. Reagan had his problems, most notably the Iran-Contra affair. But, he was able to maintain relatively cordial terms with Congressional Democrats and had a high approval rating through both terms of his presidency. Bill Clinton started out with a low approval rating, but his numbers rose steadily and matched Reagan's before the end of Clinton's first term. Like Reagan and Tip O'Neill, Clinton and House Speaker Newt Gingrich developed a productive working relationship during Clinton's first term.

Unfortunately, the good vibrations between Bill Clinton and the Republican-dominated Congress ended when the Monica Lewinsky scandal broke. Counter-intuitively, Clinton's approval rating shot up to 73% after the Republicans began impeachment proceedings. Before the Clinton impeachment, there was usually a congruence between bipartisanship within the government and presidential approval rating. If Republicans and Democrats were perceived as working together, polls showed the people approved. But the warfare which erupted between Bill Clinton and Congressional Republicans divided the country in a surprising way. Most people approved of the job Clinton did as President and disapproved of his impeachment by the Gingrich-led Republicans.

Yet, there were and are divisive repercussions related to Bill's misbehavior. That "he got away with it" still rankles Evangelical voters, who have become dependably Republican. Historically Evangelicals tended to vote Democrat and supported fellow Evangelical Jimmy Carter against Gerald Ford. They began tilting Republican after the formation of The Moral Majority by Jerry Falwell in 1979. Falwell quickly became a major political player and helped Reagan defeat Carter in 1980. The Repubs had a lock on the Evangelical vote by the time Bill Clinton left office. They favored Trump over Mrs. Clinton by a wide majority.

Hillary is a life-long church-goer. Trump has repeatedly demonstrated his lack of familiarity with the Bible and Christian practices. Yet, Christian Evangelical voters preferred a known adulterer and thrice married man rather than the woman who "stood by her man". It wasn't amore for Trump so much as animosity for the Clintons and the Democratic Party.

In 2000 when Bush beat Gore in the election decided by the Supreme Court, the Republicans hung on to a slim majority in Congress. That majority slipped away during the Bush presidency. When Obama was elected in 2008 the Democrats had majorities in both the House and Senate. But the Republicans regained control of both houses before the end of Obama's second term.

The political swings at the federal level in recent history do make American voters look rather fickle. We elect a President and give his party control of Congress at the beginning or at some point during his term. Then we become disenchanted and turn over control of Congress to the other party before the President is out of office.

Another clear trend in modern US politics that dates back to Harry Truman is the tendency to alternate the winning party of the presidency. The only exception to switching back and forth between a Republican and Democratic President since Truman is Bush Senior's one term following Reagan. (Johnson fulfilling Kennedy's first term and Ford completing Nixon's second do not count as breaking the trend, because they were not elected by the voters as the immediate successor.) So, Trump winning the election could be explained as the normal cycle of the voters taking out their dissatisfaction with the current President on the next candidate of the current President's party.

But there is a factor other than these historical voter patterns influencing recent elections and the perception of a widening chasm of distrust and dislike within US politics. That factor is the increasing power of the Tea Party within the Republican Party and the corresponding increase of influence of the Progressive Left within the Democratic Party. These voting blocs have arguably pushed the two major parties further apart on policy issues than they have been since the divide over civil rights and the Viet Nam War.

Although Kennedy started that war and Johnson escalated it, by the 1968 elections many young Democrats (Baby Boomers) had turned against the war. The hawkish Nixon promised to end the war, but it dragged on. The 1972 presidential election pitted peacenik George McGovern against war-hawk Nixon. The Democrats had become the peace party and the Republicans the war party. The Dems were pro civil rights, the Repubs anti.

That division was very clear and created even more open hostility between those on opposite sides of the issues than anything in our current politics. Abortion is as toxic a political issue as any of the current hot button issues. It generates a tremendous amount of passionate anger on both sides and has been the pretext for murder of abortion providers. But the heat it generates pales in comparison to the number of murders, demonstrations, and riots over civil rights and the Viet Nam War in the 1960's and early 70's. The current anti and pro abortion organizations are much less violent than the KKK, Black Panthers, and Weather Underground of the 1960's. There have been 11 murders and 26 attempted murders due to anti-abortion violence, according to the National Abortion Federation. As upsetting as that is, the number is minuscule compared to the hundreds who died in riots over civil rights and the war, activists killed by white supremacists and cops, and those killed by groups like the Weathermen and Symbionese Liberation Army.

When I was a child, before the civil rights and anti-war movements became such powerful political forces, I can remember adults saying there wasn't a dime's worth of difference between Kennedy and Nixon and other Democrat and Republican politicians. As a teenager, I heard grownups describe the 1968 contest between Nixon and Hubert Humphrey as a choice between "the lesser of two evils". The Depression, World War II, the need for solidarity, and FDR's charisma largely united the country through the 1930's and 40's. Even after the end of World War II northern Democrats and northern and southern Republicans found a lot of common ground on major policy issues. No wonder voters began to complain about "not a dime's worth of difference" between candidates of the opposing parties. Southern Democrats were the only regional outliers on major policy issues. They were opposed to civil right legislation and more hawkish on international relations.

But a divide began to develop after the uniting figure of Uncle Ike Eisenhower ended his presidency. It wasn't a huge factor in the Nixon/Kennedy race in 1960; but Republicans learned something from the loss. The lesson became the "southern strategy". By its successful adoption, the voting patterns of southern states completely shifted from Democrat to Republican. By 1980 the strategy helped Ronald Reagan defeat the incumbent Jimmy Carter.

Southern states had voted dependably Democrat since the Civil War. The northeastern states and California were almost as dependably

Republican. By 1980 these regions flipped, so the South was dominated by Republicans and New England and California by Democrats. Only the Great Lakes region of the Midwest remained a major battleground. Hence, the flip of Pennsylvania, Michigan, and Wisconsin from Obama to Trump is viewed as the lynch pin of Trump's victory over Hillary by the pollsters.

During the same timeline of the regional flip, rural and suburban voters began to tilt heavily toward the Republicans and urban voters toward the Democrats. African-Americans switched from Republican to Democrat in overwhelming percentages. Blue collar and older white men, even union members, have been trending away from Democrat to Republican.

Pollsters have become increasingly confident in reporting to their political clients that a statistical probability has developed among the electorate along regional/racial/gender/generational lines. The parties can almost take it for granted that the vast majority of young-female-minority voters will pull the Democratic lever, while working class and older-white-men will vote Republican in large numbers.

So-called identity politics dominated the discussions of the pundits during the last presidential election. You could not make it through a session of talking heads on TV-news channels without mention of how important it would be for each party to "turn out its base". The core of the Republican base was described as working-class-white-men and senior citizens. The Democrat core was supposedly Millennials, minorities, and some pundit/pollsters added college-educated-white-women to that mix.

How we cast our votes is determined, according to the political experts, not so much by political philosophy, as by region, race, age, education, and possibly gender. Politicians in both parties describe their party as a "big tent". The news media and pollsters tell a different story. In reality, how welcome we feel in either tent may depend on what's on our ID card as to age, race, gender, geographical area, and now, even educational level.

The polls (not the Poles) have been criticized for the inaccurate prediction of a Clinton victory in the 2016 election. So, you might think their influence will wane in future elections. The post-election evidence runs in the contrary direction. Wolf Blitzer and his crew at CNN, and the other news crews, poured over election results segmenting voters into categories of urban/rural, white/minority, Millennial/Baby Boom, college educated or not. The implicit message of this demographic and socio-economic analysis is that you are expected to vote according to your "identity", i.e., the categories that describe you.

An effect of constantly dissecting voting patterns according to identity politics is a not-so-subtle pressure to vote along with everybody else in your identity category. You're a traitor to your race if black and vote Republican. You're a traitor to your generation if a Millennial and didn't vote for Bernie Sanders. This slicing and dicing of voter demographics encourages division among voters at a different level than the intellectual challenge of judging which candidate will best serve the country. We are implicitly pressured to cast our vote based on which candidate and party best represents our particular demographic.

A statement often made by spokespersons for minority voters and minority entertainment consumers is, "I want to vote for (or watch on TV or see in the movies) *someone who looks like me*." That's certainly understandable, if people who look like you have been denied "a place at the table". Liberal Democrats, who are especially sympathetic to that plea, were not, however, so pleased to learn that working-class and older white-men also decided they wanted to vote for the candidate that looked like them in the 2016 presidential election. (No jokes please about their need for an eye exam, since the billionaire Trump doesn't look like anyone else, especially working-class guys of any age, shape, or color.)

No wonder it's gotten hard to talk about politics with people on the other side. Geographic region has played a major role in voter trends since the issue of slavery divided the states. Later, civil rights issues divided voters by race as well as region, and to some extent rural versus urban. The Viet Nam War divided voters by generation/age. Identifying statistical voter patterns along demographic lines is not new. Pollsters have recently added the category of sexual preference. What is different is the intense focus of the news media on these demographic differences in voter patterns. Voters for the other side don't just disagree with me on the issues, they aren't like me and they don't look like me.

It might have been wishful thinking, civic myth-making or just patriotic fiction, but American kids of my generation were taught in Civics Class that good citizens voted for the candidate who would best serve the country. We were not taught that loyalty was owed to our generation, race, gender, educational level, or sexual preference. It was to the nation.

In recent elections we might find ourselves pulled right or left by the ideological appeal of the Tea Party or Leftist Progressivism. That's polarization according to the traditional approach of appealing to different political philosophies and values. Those who vote according to ideological allegiance presumably believe that the country will be best served by like-minded politicians. The new and intense focus on "identity politics" divides us at another level regardless of what we think or value.

It's not just a matter of party affiliation and candidate preference, or even political philosophy. It's about who I am, not what I think or believe. It's existential.

### *Finding the Truth, Valuing Tolerant Civility, and Avoiding Hypocrisy*

Life in the virtual world has made data gathering about us much easier. When I ran for Indianapolis City Council in the Democratic Primary of 1979, the only information available to local office-seekers about voters in their district were names, addresses, and voting history. That information was compiled by the parties from the official election records of the County Clerk. Now, political candidates, parties, and Political Action Committees can obtain an incredible amount of information about voters. Our purchasing habits, hobbies, favorite books and movies -- all the personally descriptive info we post in social media and give to Amazon or Google is within the grasp of those who want to influence our vote.

Aspiring 2020 presidential candidates began gathering data about potential supporters and even purchasing online ads before the end of President Trump's first 100 days in office. Money poured in to the coffers of potential Trump opponents in unprecedented amounts through online advertising.

"When you stack it up against other ways to raise money, it has the advantage that when you're fundraising, you're also mobilizing a base that you can use for other actions," Michael Malbin, the head of the Campaign Finance Institute, told *Huff Post.* "The important thing is that these are people who might not only vote for them, but might recommend them to other people."

Campaign fundraisers say the deluge of money currently coming in online is unlike anything the party has ever seen in the first quarter following a presidential election. More than one operative described investments in digital advertising as "free money," and as a chance for someone with an eye on the White House to build a foundation for that campaign.

Sam Stein, *Huff Post,* "Potential 2020 Candidates Are Already Spending Big On Online Ads. Here's Why," May 15, 2017

Fundraising for the next presidential election only weeks into a new presidential term would have been considered ridiculous in previous political eras. The virtual reality we now inhabit not only makes digital ads possible but encourages advertisers to try to sell us 24/7/365; so why not politicians?

US voters in earlier historical eras might have been as passionate about their politics as we are now, but they were not harassed nearly as much as we are by political advertising. The emotional demands the politicos make on us is inescapable. They want us to be outraged at the latest indiscretion of President Trump. If you are upset that he disclosed classified information to the Ruskies or fired FBI Director James Comey, you might be primed to give money to a potential challenger. Or, you might be outraged that the media is engaged in a witch hunt against your President. Up pops an ad when you open Facebook or Google and there's your chance to donate to a campaign committee, political party, or PAC. Don't think about whether it makes sense to give your hard-earned cash to a potential candidate in an election almost four years away, just feel the burn and open your wallet.

Clinton v. Trump did not divide the nation as much as it was when Thomas Jefferson and Aaron Burr tied for electoral votes in 1800. Who would be our third President was only decided after 36 ballots in the House of Representatives. If that political division wasn't polarizing enough, in 1804 Burr shot Jefferson's ally Alexander Hamilton in a duel. Then, Burr began scheming against the federal government. He was tried for treason at the insistence of President Jefferson. Burr was acquitted. Candidate Trump threatened to have Hillary Clinton prosecuted and "locked up" for her emails and role in Benghazi, if he won the election. Unlike President Jefferson, President Trump didn't insist that his former rival be prosecuted. So perhaps our political differences aren't as polarizing as in the era depicted in *Hamilton.* Maybe it just feels so polarized because we are bombarded 24/7/365 with political news and campaign ads.

We are certainly not as divided as when the nation actually split during the Civil War over slavery and states' rights. Nor are divisions now as bloody as they were leading up to and after the 1968 election of Richard Nixon. Blood was shed on the streets of Watts and other cities in "race riots". There were massive demonstrations against the Viet Nam War and for civil rights. Student demonstrators (or rioters, depending on your perspective) were shot down at Kent State and Jackson State during the Johnson/Nixon era.

"Love it or leave it!" Nixon's "silent majority" not-so-silently shouted at long-haired hippies, draft-card burning anti-war protesters, bra-burning feminists, and all other "un-American" types. The young, the Left, and counter-culture advocates returned the antagonism. The demographic and cultural divisiveness that arose in the 1960s still echoes through American politics. The parallels between the Nixon and Trump campaign themes -- a patriotic call to "make America great again" -- are obvious. The allegations of conspiracy, turmoil within the Trump White House, and the appointment of a special prosecutor look familiar to those of us old enough to remember Watergate. Yes, there are historical (and psychological) parallels between Nixon and Trump.

Every political era has its divisions and its apocalyptic prophets of doom. The alt-right and some extremists on the Left may think either Obama's or Trump's election was a sign that the end-time of the USA is at hand. History indicates otherwise. We survived Watergate and, I think, became a stronger and wiser nation for it.

Allegations beyond temperamental unfitness but actual criminal conduct are mounting against President Trump as I'm writing this in May 2017. Now that Robert Mueller has been appointed Special Counsel by the Department of Justice, we may know whether crimes were committed and impeachment of the President warranted by the time this book is published. Collusion between the Russians and the Trump campaign to try to influence the outcome of the presidential election and/or the President obstructing justice by interfering in the investigation of General Michael Flynn by the FBI would certainly warrant impeachment as much as Nixon ordering a crew to burgle an office of the Democratic Party in the Watergate Building to steal documents and bug the phones. If those crimes are proved against the President, they are more egregious than Bill Clinton perjuring himself over his affair with Monica Lewinsky.

But, at least, Trump didn't shoot anyone for insulting Melania when she was accused of plagiarizing a speech by Michelle Obama at the Republican National Convention. Andrew Jackson would have. He shot and killed a political rival, Charles Dickinson, for accusing him of welching on a bet and insulting his wife. The total number of men Jackson shot in duels and disputes during the course of his political career is debated by historians. But hey, even one is more than Trump. The President's harshest critics, when calling him the worst President ever, might look back at Andrew Jackson who forced Native Americans onto the Trail of Tears. Andrew Johnson gutted Lincoln's plans for "Reconstruction" of the South after the end of the Civil War. Some historians blame that President

Johnson for the rise of the KKK, the development of Jim Crow, and turning back the tide of progress in civil rights for African-Americans. George W. Bush started two unfunded wars with economic policies (or a lack thereof) which helped trigger The Great Recession, after promising less involvement in the Middle East and a stronger economy. The US has surely survived presidents as bad as the current one. (Millard Fillmore?)

What is unique about the current political divide over President Trump is that the previous rips in the national fabric occurred before the existence of social media and 24-hour cable news. These new forms of socializing, communicating, and information dissemination allow us access to more and different contacts and content than existed in any previous era. And they make it harder to escape being sucked into the emotional maelstrom whipped up by the media.

The Internet can widen our horizons by connecting us with people we will never encounter offline. By engaging with people of different backgrounds and different points of view, our own understanding of our shared humanity is deepened. Barriers of class and culture can be breached. Or, verbal hand grenades can be hurled over those barriers. Or, we can narrow our networking and information sources to the silos that confirm our own limited and biased understanding of the world.

When communities had one newspaper and television news was limited to the three networks, it was easier to reach agreement about what the facts were relevant to a political issue. On TV there wasn't much difference in the reporting of ABC, CBS, and NBC. Newspapers all relied on the stringers of the Associated Press (AP) and United Press International (UPS) for their national and international news reports. Radio stations relied on the same sources. So "the facts" were usually not in dispute during dinner table discussions of politics and current events. What to do about the situations we learned about in the news was where political discussions tended to go.

In the age of the Internet and cable news "the facts" may be very different for Fox and MSNBC viewers. The following were the headlines about the same major story from four different online news sources on May 15, 2017:

*Washington Post*: "Trump shared classified info to Russians"

*Breitbart*: "McMaster: WaPo Classified Info Story Is 'False' – 'I Was In the Room, It Didn't Happen'"

*Slate*: "The Astonished Responses to Trump's Leak of Classified Intel to the Russians"

***Daily Mail:*** "Security Advisor McMaster furiously DENIES Trump leaked 'highly classified' information to the Russians"

Did President Trump leak classified information to the Russians? What you "knew" from reading/watching/listening to the news on the day the story broke would depend on your news source. How to interpret the facts and what to do about it are secondary and tertiary challenges. The first is to try to figure out what actually happened. News consumers that only read *Slate* may think they know whether the President leaked info to the Ruskies or not. So will those who only read the ***Daily Mail.***

But it's all out there on the Internet. Both sides of a story, as well as sources that actually aim for neutrality and objectivity in reporting, can be accessed. I think the three old grandmas of television news, ABC, CBS, and NBC, as well as PBS and NPR, sincerely try to present objective-neutral reporting. The cable networks interlace commentary and opinion so much with their news reporting it is difficult to disassociate fact from conjecture, reporting from editorializing.

If you have Facebook friends with diverse political views, you can receive and share as much cross-cutting sourced information as you can stand. Your own Facebook network can be a way to balance your understanding of what's happening in the world. If you only have like-minded friends, your understanding of what's happening and why is probably imbalanced and distorted.

A popular counter-cultural slogan of the 1960's was: "Yeah man, we've got freedom of the press – if you can afford to own a newspaper."

Social media allows everybody to act like a newspaper. Anyone who wants to can post articles and disseminate information. And it really is free (so long as you have access to the Internet).

In his August 27, 2015 post announcing the milestone of more than one billion users logging on to Facebook in a single day, Mark Zuckerberg included this saccharine-sounding note:

> I'm so proud of our community for the progress we've made. Our community stands for giving every person a voice, for promoting understanding and for including everyone in the opportunities of our modern world.
>
> A more open and connected world is a better world. It brings stronger relationships with those you love, a stronger economy with more opportunities, and a stronger society that reflects all of our values.

But Zuckerberg is right. There's no guaranty anyone will listen, but Facebook does give every user a voice. It has absolutely created a more connected world. Unfortunately, it is too often used for purposes other than to create "a stronger society that reflects our values". (We might also note that it's not clear from his post which values Mr. Zuckerberg is referring to beyond inclusion and freedom of expression.)

Physician and social scientist Nicholas Christakis gave a TED Talk about social networks and how their structures influence behavior, which was broadcast on my local NPR station, WFYI, in May 2017. Christakis made the point that, "Networks have value ... our experience of the world depends on the social networks we're in." He went on to describe how "structurally influential people can foster the spread of cooperation or inhibit cooperation throughout a population." Christakis cited a research project involving 60 million Facebook users, and other studies, as proof that the proper use of social network systems can spread positive values out from influential leaders to the members in their networks. He said, "The spread of good and valuable things depends on social networks."

Christakis claimed that his research affirms what Mark Zuckerberg implied, that health, government, the economy, and other human relationships and systems can be improved by participation in social networks when the networks are influenced by the right people. When influenced by bad people, bad things spread.

Scholars and sages have traditionally sought and urged the rest of us to seek the truth. We won't find it on particular issues if we only look to slanted sources. And we won't help others find it if we spread biased accounts through our networks.

If you do value finding the truth, how do you, for example, determine whether President Trump leaked classified intelligence to the Russians or not? It helps to access more than one news source, and then weigh the evidence presented by each. Which relied on the most credible sources? Which tracks best with common sense and logic? It also helps to network with people who have different opinions about the President before making a judgment.

I have friends that act like they are going to barf at the mention of Fox News and others with a similar reaction to MSNBC. But they never watch the news shows preferred by "the other side"! And now, they want to gather into collectives of the like-minded on Facebook.

These ardent progressive and proud Tea Party friends of mine think they know what the other side values and believes in. But, unless you participate in a social network which includes people with views opposing your own, the assumptions you make about "them" might be inaccurate. The refusal to access news with an editorial slant contrary to our own political alignment might allow us to avoid a bout of nausea, but it leaves us ignorant of what those with opposing views "know" about our shared world.

The ability to network with people of every point of view through social media is historically unprecedented. If we are going to reduce the poisonous level of polarization, it requires us, the people, the voters, social media users, to take responsibility to seek out information from sources other than the ones which make us feel good by confirming our biases. We are more knowledgeable and we are better people for including in our social networks online and offline those with whom we disagree.

When we actually understand why people differ with us about significant issues, they will be more human to us. When we respect each other as fellow human beings we may be able to build a bridge to cross the chasm of ignorance and misunderstanding.

When I was a child, it didn't seem odd to me that my Nixon-supporting Republican parents were best of friends with our Democrat Kennedy-supporting neighbors, the Browards. I listened to my father and mother eviscerate Kennedy and the Democrats over the dinner table. My best friend, Bubby Broward, tried to convince me that his parents were right; Dick Nixon would be a terrible President. Yet, our parents belonged to the same church, the same social circle and civic clubs. They regularly partied together and knew they could depend on each other should any need arise. Bubby and I played together every day without any disruption due to the grown-ups' political differences.

Bubby and I were born in 1953 and grew up together in the small city of Goshen, Indiana. Disagreements about politics did not seem to interfere with personal relationships in the adult world of our childhood. We might look back on small-town middle-America of the late 1950's and early 60's as myopic from our current vantage point. It was definitely more segregated by race. Goshen had one black resident, a Goshen College professor. We had a few Hispanic residents, but most were transients working the farm fields outside town. Our one Jewish family was prominent within the business community and social life of the town.

My father and his friends joined private clubs, like the Elks, Moose, and Eagles. Protestants joined the Masons and Catholics joined the Knights of Columbus. The wives were members of social sororities and auxiliary clubs. I suppose these associations were the 1950's and 60's version of like-minded collectives. But they weren't based on political ideologies. Members of the K of C and Masons would have thought it bizarre if someone suggested they shouldn't or couldn't talk politics with members of the other club.

The danger of losing the value of tolerance within our social networks is that our experience of human reality atrophies. It's a very odd development that progressives trumpet the value of diversity in race, ethnicity, religion, gender, and sexual orientation louder than ever. Yet, many liberal trumpeters want to limit the ideological and political diversity within their social-media networks. If a friend or follower posts irritating comments about a political issue, how quick are we to pull the trigger to block or unfriend them? Why put up with people we disagree with when it's so easy to avoid them? A demand for purity in the political thought and expression of others smacks of the intolerance of fascist and Marxist organizations.

On Twitter I've read the most ghastly, obnoxious, and insulting posts mean-nasty minds are capable of creating. Trolling and attacking are extracurricular activities for some and an occupation for others. We ought to kick out of our networks anyone who engages in that sort of despicable online behavior. No one should put up with intentionally offensive use of social media. On the other hand, shouldn't we have skin thick enough to tolerate political posts by friends we disagree with?

The virtual world in which we now live has changed the rules of civility and respect. The Browards and the Rasleys liked each other, despite political differences. We lived in a community that expected neighbors and friends to respect political differences. Disagreements were not hidden, but they didn't jeopardize friendships.

Now, lest old farts become too rhapsodical about the pre-Internet utopia of our youth, we should not forget how easy it is to access information and purchase desired goods and services on the Internet. Want to find out something you're not quite sure of, Google it. Need something you don't want to leave home to shop for, buy it on Amazon. Want to watch a movie or TV show you missed, download it from Netflix. The Internet has made life easier and more interesting.

Also, admittedly the sweet bye and bye might not have been so sweet if you weren't white. But venerating certain traditional values, like civility and tolerance of different political opinions, does not require an acceptance of other forms of intolerance from the past. Those traditional values are not at odds with and can complement progressive values, like inclusivity and diversity.

Civility, tolerance, inclusivity, diversity, and freedom of expression, these might be the values Mark Zuckerberg was alluding to in his August 27, 2015 FB post lauding the accomplishments of Facebook. If we apply those values to our social networking, life will be better for us and our friends. And, we won't be hypocrites when we claim to value diversity and inclusivity.

## *Passionate Intolerance and Waste of a Valuable Resource*

Tea Party sympathizers were furious while Obama was President. Progressives are now furious that Trump is President. It is infuriating when you are absolutely sure your candidate is better than her opponent, and then the other guy wins. How could anyone have been so stupid as to vote for Obama!? How can you possibly justify voting for Trump!? But, so it goes. No one wins all the time. We often don't get what we want in life. So why have Americans become so furious when our preferred candidate loses? Why are we taking it so personally and why are we holding it against those who disagreed with us and voted for the candidate we opposed?

An anti-Trump FB friend, Ron, explained his fury that Trump won in his response to my invitation to participate in the experiment on my Facebook page:

You ask does the other side have the right to hold an opposing view. Sure as long as they don't act on it. But elections have consequences. Elections kill people. ...

So, it's okay with Ron to disagree with him, but you shouldn't vote or act in opposition to his Progressive beliefs. If you do, you may be responsible for killing people.

American voters should be passionate about their politics. Those who are so passionate as to think which candidate wins may be a life or death decision are invested in our democracy as I've advocated in this book. Ron is an informed and conscientious voter. He is a blue-collar-older-white guy who voted for Sanders in the Democratic Primary and Clinton in the general election. He did not vote consistent with the statistical prediction of pollsters according to his "identity". Ron takes his responsibility to vote for the best candidate very seriously. But wait a minute – the other side has the right to hold an opposing view but not to act on it!? That is the antithesis of democracy.

My Progressive friend is guilty of a sin similar to the one William Deresiewiez described in his *American Scholar* article quoted above. "If you are using your speech to try to silence speech, you are not in favor of free speech. You are only in favor of yourself." My FB friend has not gone so far as to demand Tea Partiers be silent; they just shouldn't act on their beliefs. If they don't have the right to act on their beliefs, then they might as well be silent. Isn't that what follows in the logic of this intolerant sort of thinking?

I know him personally, so I am sure that Ron would not do this, but attacking, insulting, trolling your opponents in social media can be justified as your righteous duty, if you truly feel your opponents are responsible for killing people because of who they voted for. Your moral righteousness is like that of the Holy Roman Inquisition. Heretics should be tortured into acceptance that they are wrong and confess their error, or keep silent. Social media trolls don't have the ability to physically torture, so they harass and harry their opponents.

In the US we like to think of our nation as a light unto the world for freedom, diversity, and tolerance. These values are enshrined in the sacred-secular documents created by our founding fathers. The US is also the cradle of technological innovation. This is where the Internet and social media were created, for god's sake. One might have expected that the revolution in communications technology would have reached a pinnacle of noble purpose here in the US. Trough the new media we could find ways to promote the fundamental values of our great nation, right? Or, we can make the dominant uses the sale of products, posting selfies and silly videos, and engaging in angry rants.

Social media was an important tool used by activists in the Green Revolution in Iran and the Arab Spring. Subversive use of social media by opponents to authoritarian states may have fallen short of instigating successful revolutions against repressive governments in the Middle East, but it has been a thorn in their sides and a catalyst for reform. It offers one of the few means activists can express dissent against totalitarian regimes. That's why authoritarian states, like China and Russian, try to stifle opposition on social media. But they haven't been able to stamp it out entirely.

Given these ennobling examples in other countries, isn't it kind of embarrassing that here in the US we'd rather post cat videos?

During the Clinton v. Trump campaign season I became increasingly aware of a tendency to say things on social media that I would not say to a person face-to-face. When I saw a pro-Trump or anti-Clinton post that irritated me, I immediately felt an impulse to respond quickly and angrily. It was hard to restrain; and sometimes I didn't bother. I gave in to expressing myself more angrily than I would in the actual presence of others. It felt good to let it out in that moment of self-righteous outrage.

It took awhile, but distaste began to develop for using social media as a means to blast insults and ridicule political opponents. The original temptation was like eating sweets or fast food. There was an immediate reward, but I knew it wasn't good for my long-term health. Nevertheless, even as a residual ickiness began to build up, I kept doing it on Twitter. I often "liked" those who did it on Facebook and sometimes left a snarky comment of my own. Even though I was beginning to dislike what I saw in the proverbial mirror, I found, as Saint Paul admonished, the spirit was strong but the flesh weak.

I began to wonder whether others were experiencing a similar dissatisfaction with their experiences in social media. I wondered whether some of my FB friends might be interested in trying to curb these unsavory tendencies and use Facebook for a higher and better use.

The feeling of ickiness about my own occasional use of Facebook and Twitter was a primary motivation in deciding to ask Facebook friends whether they would join in an effort to engage in civil discourse about controversial political topics. Could we overcome the temptation to be uncivil while the atmosphere of social media was still polluted by the toxicity of the Clinton v. Trump election?

# IV. Can't We All Just Get Along?

"I just want to say - you know - can we all get along? Can we, can we get along? Can we stop making it horrible for the older people and the kids? ... I mean please, we can, we can get along here. We all can get along - we just gotta, we gotta. I mean, we're all stuck here for a while, let's, you know let's try to work it out, let's try to beat it, you know, let's try to work it out." Rodney King, May 1, 1992

### *The Experiment*

Near the end of February 2017, after Trump had been President for just over one month, I began an experiment on Facebook. The wound of Clinton's defeat, and the triumph of Trump's election, were still fresh.

During the last week of February and the first two weeks of March I posted on my Facebook page a series of discussion topics about "hot" political issues. I invited friends with different political views to respond, but requested they reply civilly to those with whom they disagreed. It was an experiment to see if civil discourse is still possible on Facebook. (Twitter is too far gone.)

I was curious to discover what, if any, responses the posts would generate. Would Facebook friends even be willing to participate in a political discussion-thread with an expectation that they treat political opponents with respect? Would they be capable of complying with a requirement of civility? Would anyone unfriend me for attempting to create such a forum or for my own posts on the topics in the threads? I planned to be the facilitator and to contribute my own comments in the discussion threads.

### *My Qualifications and the Temptation to Scream and Run Away*

I am not a techie or social media maven, but I am regularly on one or another social network. I rarely use Google+; just an occasional post of a book review or reading another contributor's book review. I do the same on Goodreads with a little more frequency. Occasionally I read an article posted by a contact in LinkedIn. If I notice a promotion or employment anniversary on LinkedIn, I might send a note of congratulations. I've never used Instagram or Snapchat. As mentioned, I've used Twitter to vent and to try to take the pulse of the US and international community on issues of interest. My initial interest in Twitter was to promote the books I've written and to seek financial support for a nonprofit I founded (Basa Village Foundation). I slowly developed over 13,000 Twitter followers. My use of Twitter significantly declined after Trump's inauguration.

Facebook was and still is my preferred social media network. I check in almost every day. I have just over 680 FB friends. Most of whom I was connected with in some way before we friended each other on Facebook. I do accept friend requests from people I've not met offline, so long as it appears they do not have ulterior motives of a commercial nature and their identity is authentic.

My qualifications to facilitate civil discussions among Facebook friends are from experiences outside social media. I served as an advocate or mediator in more mediations and settlement conferences than I can count in my 30 years of practicing law. I also sat as a pro tem judge several times. I took counseling courses to acquire a Master of Divinity degree, and I have taught a seminar course on philanthropy at Marian University and Butler University as an adjunct instructor. Before I was one, I taught a course through Oasis to help older adults cope with life changes. And, before teaching regular university classes I taught a course about the culture of Nepal for the IUPUI Extended Education Program.

*Newsweek Magazine* published an article I wrote about the "revolutionary transformation" of the legal system by the implementation of mediation as an alternative to litigation. My book, *Godless - Living a Valuable Life beyond Beliefs*, analyzes different methods of dispute resolution. So, I've spent a significant amount of time and effort involved with, thinking about, and writing about mediating disputes.

But the most relevant experience for facilitating a Facebook discussion thread was serving as the leader/facilitator of adult discussion groups at two different churches. One was Presbyterian, the other Quaker.

The weekly discussions in the church classes were about current topics in the news or significant religious and political issues. Religious and political persuasions covered a wide spectrum in each class. In the Quaker class one member was an atheist-socialist and another was a rightwing evangelical-Christian. In both classes we typically had a range of views, but members felt comfortable and safe to express disagreement with each other. I served as leader/facilitator of each class for several years. My leadership of the Presbyterian class was during the younger Bush years, the Quaker class during the Obama years.

Within the Quaker class, the intensity and passion expressed by conservative Republicans and Tea Party sympathizers began to escalate noticeably during Obama's second term. So did the response of progressive Democrats, just like on social media.

During the campaign season of 2016 a rightwing Republican left the Quaker class never to return. The last time he attended the class, he growled at the left-wingers, "You people don't live in the real world." The majority of class members were liberal Democrats, but there were several regular attendees who were conservative Republicans. By the end of the Obama Presidency several other conservative members had drifted away from the class. The most conservative religious/political member of the class started a short-lived alternative class.

My experience with the Presbyterian class during the George W. Bush years followed a similar pattern. Like the Quakers, Presbyterian members of the class with contrary views actively participated for several years. There were passionate disagreements, but no one got so upset as to leave the group. And then one day it changed.

A liberal-feminist member vented her spleen after an evangelical member of the class expressed concern about the sympathetic direction the denomination was moving on "gay rights". She said, without mentioning his name or speaking directly to him, that opposing gay rights within the church was "stupid". She knew very well that other members of the class were opposed to the ordination of gay Presbyterians. The conservative members of the class quit the next week and started their own class.

There were two identifiable factors in the fracturing of the community of both classes. They each occurred during a very divisive period, and an uncivil statement was made about members. For the Presbyterians the split occurred while the denomination was forced to decide where it stood on gay rights. Many Presbyterians left the denomination as it moved toward allowing ordination of gay ministers and ceasing to consider homosexuality as a state of sin. Departures from the Quaker class began toward the end of Obama's second term and the beginning of the 2016 presidential campaign. In each case a left/right division was creating more tension within the group, and there was a breach of the unspoken rule of civility: indirectly calling members "stupid" for opposing gay rights in the Presby class, and "You people don't live in the real world" in the Friends class.

The breakup of the classes caused some pain and perplexity. They are examples outside social media of the human tendency to avoid conflict and to silo. In each of those cases, however, members with opposing political/religious views met and discussed controversial issues for years before the break-up. And, relationships outside of the classes were not severed. The class members remained within their churches. They continued worshipping together and participating in other church activities without any apparent animosity.

The splintering of the church classes happened without members hurling personal insults beyond the one incident in each case. Neither of those insults was directed exactly at one member by another. They were very mild compared to the ugly ad hominem comments I've seen posted in social media by users who get into political or religious squabbles. Some interpersonal relations within the church communities were strained temporarily. But then, members moved on despite their differences, similar to how my parents and our neighbor-friends, the Browards, handled their political disagreements.

Siloing is not a new phenomenon in human relations. It's an old tendency. It's just easier to practice in social media.

When I was studying denominationalism in seminary in the mid 1980s, I learned that there were over 800 Christian denominations in Indiana. Amazing! In just one medium-size state, Christians felt the need to divide into that many different denominations. Most were started over some arcane doctrinal disagreement. Say, a member has a revelation that "the body and blood of Christ" shared in Communion is symbolic, not actually Jesus' body and blood. The denominational authorities refuse to recognize the revelation and won't change the official doctrine of transubstantiation. So, that member leaves and starts a new church with fellow dissidents.

Social media has created a new way to follow this age-old pattern of behavior. It's much easier to scream and run away from groups and break relationships. You don't have to look the person, who was your friend and now your nemesis, in the eye. When it's not face-to-face, it takes little courage to terminate a relationship. It's more tempting to use rude language toward those with whom we disagree when we're not in the same room with them. It's easier to duck the challenge of rationally responding to expressions of opinions contrary to our own, when we can just log off.

A few minutes online and you can attack people of different persuasions from your own. With a couple clicks you can block or delete comments you don't like. And, you can unfriend anyone whose comments irritate you. But, giving in to these temptations results in a narrowing of our exposure to diverse opinions and sources of information.

The Internet offers an amazing cornucopia of information, perspectives, and points of view. Social media can be a trailhead to commence a treasure hunt to widen and deepen our knowledge of the world. It can also be a shell in which we hide from the world by only sharing with like-minded friends.

Life is more pleasant not to have your opinions challenged. I well understand this. I have left two different churches, in part, because I disagreed with the theology being promoted. My theology, or lack thereof, ceased to fit comfortably with church doctrine in one case and with the pastor's preaching in the other. It wasn't easy to leave in either case. But it seemed easier than to stay and advocate for a minority point of view within each church.

So yes, life is more comfortable when we can avoid confrontation with opinions that contrast with our own, when our reasoning and analysis is left unchallenged, and our conclusions uncontradicted. Socrates claimed that, "The unexamined life is not worth living." He died a martyr for free thinkers and the cause of rational discourse. He would be wagging his finger at our weak and cowardly inclination to avoid confrontation and only hang out with friends who affirm us.

## *Health Benefits of Accepting Challenges*

According to The National Institute of Diabetes and Digestive and Kidney Diseases, "More than one-third (35.7 percent) of adults are considered to be obese. More than 1 in 20 (6.3 percent) have extreme obesity. Almost 3 in 4 men (74 percent) are considered to be overweight or obese."

Social media has arisen coincident with a dramatic obesity rate increase in the US and worldwide. Many of us living in the digitized world are not compelled to physically exercise. We can live much of our lives comfortably seated in front of a screen or with a device in hand. While sitting comfortably in front of a screen, why not indulge ourselves further by eating fat-laden food and drinking sugar-laced beverages?

Americans have grown soft and obese, because we don't want to be challenged to get off our fat asses to exercise. We don't like to be challenged to stop eating all the delicious-tasting but unhealthy foods and beverages so quick and easy to purchase and consume. We can passively consume entertainment content and play video games for stimulation while munching on trans-fat saturated foods and sipping soda pop. Heart rates of couch potatoes might reach their zenith when they are hammering out nasty diatribes on keyboards during a social media rant.

It's cheap too. Internet access has become like the heat and light bill. It's a basic necessity of life. So, once that cost is covered to go on social media and spend a couple hours costs nothing, except the time spent. Going to the opera, art museum, current or classic cinema, or a sporting event costs good money. Much cheaper and easier to stay home and spend the evening Facebooking, tweeting, Instagramming, or Snapchatting than to go out, pay for transportation or parking, and a ticket to a cultural event.

Sorry to sound like a self-righteous scold, but a lifestyle lived primarily through a screen and keyboard is surely contributing as much to the obesity epidemic as fast foods and sugary beverages.

Our intellectual and emotional muscles grow weak and slack, if they are not refined through aesthetic encounters with beauty and tested by confronting new and different ideas. Just being challenged to explain and defend a position taken strengthens our intellectual muscles.

The ability to develop a coherent argument to support a position in a friendly debate should be an enjoyable test of the strength of your position. But pleasure in that kind of intellectual give and take seems to be waning as political polarization drives us into opposing camps that don't want to communicate with each other. Political polarization contributes to the obesity epidemic by promoting fat-headedness.

Okay, I am coming off as a self-righteous scold, but I can't help it. I'm descended from Puritans on my mother's side. But there is a theme which relates siloing with like-minded FB friends, avoiding physical exercise, watching only the news stations that confirm our prejudices, and eating junk food. It's a cheap and easy way to live.

Life is more comfortable in the short run when we take the easy way, the least challenging route. Of course we want to sit in the most comfortable chair and sleep on the most comfortable mattress. The drive to seek comfort is a basic aspect of human nature. But the people we admire most temper that drive with the desire to grow, to be strong, to be tested, to achieve and excel.

The good life, as many ancient Greek philosophers taught, is found in balance. Finding a balance of challenging physical and mental exercise on one side of the scales, with a comfortable lifestyle on the other, is difficult. It's especially difficult for hardworking folks. After the stress of a work day, it's tempting just to tuck in with comfort food, a glass of wine or beer, and non-stressful online experiences or a TV show. I've spent many hours that way.

Socrates and his followers would counter that point with this: The good life is not supposed to be easy. You have to strive to find it. The Athenian law-giver, Solon, is credited with the saying, "Count no man happy until he is dead." Seeking the balance of a good life is a life-long pursuit of refinement. In Plato's account of Socrates' death in **The Phaedo**, Socrates was still challenging his disciples to examine philosophical issues right up until the moment he drank the poisonous hemlock. He died doing what he loved.

I am no Socrates and I certainly did not want to be condemned for trying to promote civil discourse about political issues. But, I did think it would be worth the risk of being unfriended to try the experiment on Facebook. Maybe it would inspire some of my FB friends to examine how they are using social media. They might conclude that it has a higher and better use than angry ranting and narcissic blathering.

# V. Barbarism or Civility; The Choice is Ours

*Contempt for reason and science leads in the end to barbarism – its necessary consequence being the rudest superstition, and sheer helplessness in the presence of all sorts of delusion.*

Entry on "Neo-Platonism", ***The Encyclopedia Britannica Dictionary of Arts, Sciences, and General Literature***, 9th Edition, Volume XVII, 1884

## *Civilizing the Virtual World*

Social media offers a multitude of opportunities for verbal fencing to toughen the mind and improve writing skills. Pick most any topic and you can probably find a page or thread which addresses it. Or, you can start your own. What I proposed to do was not entirely unique. However, no one I knew of was trying to promote rational political discourse on their own FB page. The political discussions I had encountered in Facebook were threads that developed in response to articles on sponsored pages. I wanted to encourage the development of civil discussion among citizens on their own time and in their own spaces.

Discussion boards sponsored by politicians, political parties, PACs, or news organizations all have their purposes. Their purposes tend to be commercial or to promote political interests. Passionate argumentation is usually encouraged instead of reasoned discussion. My intent was to try to promote free and open, but civil, debate among private citizens. There would be nothing to gain for anyone, except, I hoped, a better understanding of those with different views.

This would certainly require some encouragement and possibly some scolding. Because thoughtful articulation of a response to a post that challenges our conventional thinking takes time and discipline. It's much easier to blast away in the heat of the moment or post mindless platitudes. An example from one of my discussion threads:

L: IMPEACH!

T: More Bullshit !

B: Stock markets doing well, if you put your house for sale, be prepared to move, businesses, at least in our area, can't get enough help, or get it done fast enough, they're trying to fix health care, and this time we can discuss it, illegal immigration ...See More

T: They will make up anything to discredit Trump. I'm behind him 100 %

B: Aren't you supposed to support your government, including the President, even if he wasn't your choice? It's worked pretty good for decades.

T: Damn right ! ! I like it !!

B: Hell of a lot better than working for 20 cents an hour and supporting a goofy little bastard with bad hair who's sole purpose in life is to blow shit up. Or having babies for the purpose to grow up to the age where they can shoot a gun, or blow themsel...*See More*

T: Give em hell B!! I'm behind you all the way !

B: It's a waste of air. Sometimes you just get tired of hearing the same old disrespectful comments from people you have always considered respectful. Problem solvers, creating problems.

J: I am not understanding why you think this is all fake news. Trump admitted to Lester Holt he fired Comey because of the Russian investigation. He has admitted he discussed classified information with Russia. Do you not understand the implications of these things? Obviously he doesn't either, but these are serious lapses in judgement.

B: I have never liked the term "fake news". It's more like "selective news". He could say, today's a beautiful day, 90°, sunshine, and a lite breeze. Breaking  news. Today Trump said it's too hot to be outside, and if you do, he hopes you get sunburn and possibly skin cancer, and the high winds will blow your dress up and leave you at risk of being assaulted by dirty old rich men.

T: Give em hell !! You are RIGHT !!

R: Your support for the President seems unequivocal. Is there any mistake he could make that you think he could be criticized for?

T: Turning his back to the veterans or letting the liberal idiots have their way for another four years.

The topic of the discussion thread was the allegation that President Trump had released classified information to Russian officials. After the experiment ended I continued posting topics for post-experiment discussions. What is copied and pasted above is a sub-thread that developed in that post-experiment discussion. L's comment of "IMPEACH!"

prompted T's reply of "More Bullshit!", which instigated the string of replies. The main thread was more edifying.

B, R, and J were engaged in an actual discussion, but the comments of L and especially T are examples of just blasting away without contributing to the discussion other than stating antipathy or support for President Trump. T's final comment includes the uncivil "liberal idiots".

Thankfully, there were many more examples of participants engaging in serious colloquy in the experimental threads. Most of the respondents actually thought before posting a comment. But there were plenty of comments during the experiment that were mindless, impulsive replies like T's.

When confronted with a post or tweet that pisses you off, like "IMPEACH!" or "More Bullshit!", the natural inclination is to hammer out an angry reply. The offending commenter can't spit in your face or slap you. So what's the risk in mocking or insulting her? The parking brake of good manners is off. The normal desire of wanting to be perceived as a good and decent fellow within the community isn't as strong in the virtual world as in direct personal relationships. Community isn't as real, it's virtual.

Some people are just as coarse offline as online. These types don't operate with the normal impulse control of well-mannered and respectable folks. (Some would put Donald Trump in that "basket of deplorables" and use his tweets as evidence. E.g., "Donald J. Trump @realDonaldTrump Obama is, without question, the WORST EVER president. I predict he will now do something really bad and totally stupid to show manhood! 9:07 PM - 5 Jun 2014".) I often catch myself beginning to pound out an angry-impulsive response when I'm incensed by a comment in Facebook. I quit regularly reading my Twitter feed after Trump's inauguration, because I was so sick and tired of getting sucked into the sound and fury of pro and anti Trump tweets. On Facebook, I've felt the need to edit comments just posted, and regretted some I didn't edit.

I am not unique in responding with less emotional control on social media than offline. A number of people have admitted to me that they've posted/commented/tweeted things they would never have said to a person's face. How often do you actually yell, or see others yelling, at a friend who said something disagreeable? In person, we're more likely to laugh it off, politely state our disagreement, or try to better understand where the guy is coming from. We care about what others think of us and our reputation. But the risk of harm to reputation or loss of good standing feels less substantial in social media communities. We do care about what people think of us in the virtual world, just not as much.

Dory has one of the sweetest personalities of all my offline friends. But I've read replies she's posted in Facebook to comments of Trump supporters that seem like a completely different person wrote them. Her tone in some of these posts is angry, sharp, and vicious. Jake is a kind and gentle person, but I've read comments he's posted about Hillary Clinton and her supporters that are mean-spirited and crude. Dory and Jake are kind, courteous, and thoughtful in every encounter I've had with them in person. Their virtual personalities are quite different than their offline ones. A darker side of their personalities is released within the virtual world.

Social media relationships are usually not as deep and meaningful as those we have with people offline. Authentic friendships do develop through social media, but they are the exception, not the rule. There is a qualitative difference in the authenticity of a relationship lived mainly in person than one mediated by a screen and keyboard. All the love emojis we digitally send do not convey what a hug and kiss do for us. If we really care about someone we've met online, we will probably try to get together offline if possible.

Alice related to me that she is much happier since her employer let her work online. She has much greater freedom from management. Her work hours are more flexible. She can travel to Ireland, put in her minimally required time in the virtual office, and still get paid. Alice also told me that she's not even sure who else works in her department and only "knows" one of her co-workers. In a "real" office, she'd at least be able to identify everyone in her department and would probably know several other employees. Working online has its advantages, but it significantly diminishes any sense of community and comradeship within an office.

The intangible, or virtual, reality of social media grants a sense of liberation from traditional social norms and customs of behavior. It's become a license to use language we wouldn't use in direct personal relationships. Because we're operating in a different space and time from our correspondents in social media, social customs have developed which are different from those we follow when we're in the same room with others. We feel freer to insult and ridicule, and to run away if we feel ashamed of what we posted. It's not so easy to leave your family, neighborhood, school, clique, church, club, or sports team as it is to unfriend a FB friend or block a Twitter follower.

You actually have to share air and look into the eyes of your co-worker, classmate, or teammate tomorrow, if you abuse him today. Not so in a virtual community. You can drop out without a good-bye, and you can drop friends and followers without any explanation.

Civilization has tempered the primitive instincts of fight and flight, so that good and decent folks try to deal civilly with each other. Even when a friend says something stupid or disagreeable, we don't usually get in that person's face about it. We tend to be the most politely careful around people we just met or don't know well. We might "let our hair down and get real" with family and good friends, but we generally try to be on our best behavior around new acquaintances and people we don't know well.

Social media has flipped these norms. It is people we just encountered on Facebook or Twitter that we are most likely to blast, if they post something disagreeable. Who cares if I insult Vic on Facebook, when I don't expect to run across him in person? If he snarks back at me, I can bark even louder back at him or just defriend him.

If Vic is on my volleyball team, I'll make an effort to get along with him. Even though our relationship is limited to playing on the same team, I expect to see him every week through the season. When Vic makes an asinine comment during a break in practice, I might make fun of what he said or just ignore it. There are a number of socially acceptable tactics I would probably employ before feeling driven to rudely insult a teammate. On Facebook, I might give in to the instinctive reaction to call Vic a jerk or a dick, if he posted something asinine or offensive. If he comes back at me, I can just unfriend him. But it's not so easy to terminate a relationship with Vic, if he's on my team, in my club, a member of my church, or my uncle.

For those of us old enough not to take the Internet for granted, social media still seems miraculous. Wow! I just made a new friend online who lives in Rwanda. The trade-off is that I spend less time in the physical presence of other friends. The screen and keyboard as a port of entry into the virtual world of the Internet gives me access to people I will never see in person. The screen and keyboard also create a barrier of impersonal distance. That barrier lets me rashly say (type) things to others I wouldn't say in person.

Go online and look at a comment thread of sports fans. If I gave in to the temptation to post a reply to Vic's asinine post calling him a dick that would be pretty mild on some sports pages. You'll read the meanest, nastiest hair on fire comments about athletes, coaches, referees, and other commenters you can imagine in threads of passionate sports fans. Civilizing filters fall off when we enter the virtual world.

What would be helpful is for a Ms. Manners to become influential in the virtual world. Development of customs and norms of courtesy within social media would make it a more inviting and civilized medium of communal sharing.

A fundamental ethic could be as simple as do not insult or ridicule another user, unless you are insulted or ridiculed. A secondary rule could be not to interpret criticism of someone you admire or support (e.g., political candidates and office holders or entertainment and sports stars) as a personal attack on you. Why react with protective ferocity when someone you don't really know criticizes your favorite hockey player? If these two simple rules were generally followed, the virtual world would be a more pleasant place to visit where more meaningful interactions took place.

Virtual-reality barbarity does not come without cost. Donald Trump's addiction to tweeting is Exhibit 'A'. Maybe it helped him win the election, but the President's bizarre late-night and early morning tweeting has confused allies and enemies and caused diplomatic flaps.

Take Justine Sacco as Exhibit 'B'. She tweeted: "Going to Africa. Hope I don't get AIDS. Just kidding. I'm white!" She was in-flight to Cape Town, South Africa. Her snarky impulsiveness changed her life and not in a positive way.

> Sacco's Twitter feed had become a horror show. "In light of @Justine-Sacco disgusting racist tweet, I'm donating to @care today" and "How did @JustineSacco get a PR job?! Her level of racist ignorance belongs on Fox News. #AIDS can affect anyone!" and "I'm an IAC employee and I don't want @JustineSacco doing any communications on our behalf ever again. Ever." And then one from her employer, IAC, the corporate owner of The Daily Beast, OKCupid and Vimeo: "This is an outrageous, offensive comment. Employee in question currently unreachable on an intl flight." The anger soon turned to excitement: "All I want for Christmas is to see @JustineSacco's face when her plane lands and she checks her inbox/voicemail" and "Oh man, @JustineSacco is going to have the most painful phone-turning-on moment ever when her plane lands" and "We are about to watch this @JustineSacco bitch get fired. In REAL time. Before she even KNOWS she's getting fired."
> Jon Ronson, *The New York Times Magazine*, "How One Stupid Tweet Blew Up Justine Sacco's Life," Feb. 12, 2015

She was fired and went into hiding. Her South African family had a long tradition of being on the liberal side of racial politics. An aunt told Justine that her disgusting tweet was a stain on the whole family.

Her tweet was stupid and thoughtless. I'm sure Ms. Sacco would not have made that same remark to a group of strangers -- probably not to friends either -- in person. The mob-fury her tweet provoked would not have been so hateful and furious, if the tweeters knew Justine. She is, by accounts of friends, a bit silly at times, but not at all racist.

The barrier of civility social media brings down opens the gate for barbaric mob behavior. It's easy to get riled up and pile on. In fact, it feels good to be released from the restraints of polite behavior to instigate or join a mob. No cop is going to beat me with a billy club for ranting at someone on Facebook. I won't get arrested for disturbing the peace by hurling F-bombs at my political nemeses on Twitter.

The keyboard also reduces authentic intimacy in human relations. Great poets and prose writers can convey the most sublime and disgusting experiences, thoughts, and feelings with words. We regular FB users are not Wordsworths or even word smiths. Some are more gifted with the written word than others, but whatever your level of sophistication with a keyboard you have many more tools to convey feelings, thoughts, and ideas when you are in the physical presence of those you are trying to communicate with. Your tone of voice, eye movement, facial expression, gestures, a touch, the tilt of your head, arching an eyebrow, all the different forms of body language and vocal expressions convey meaning that is very difficult to duplicate through a keyboard, if you're not a gifted poet.

Talking on the phone is more intimate and expressive than communicating through a keyboard. We can try to simulate tone of voice using capitols, underlining, boldface, exclamation and question marks. But note that these are all intensifiers. They're pretty good at expressing anger, shock, and outrage. They are not as effective at more pleasant and subtle feelings.

Emojis and emoticons are weak attempts to simulate emotive communication more directly than typed words. They are a very small step in reducing the difference in physical and expressive space between the virtual and "real" worlds.

Because we lose so many tools for subtle and deeper communication, different customs and norms have necessarily developed in social media than older forms of communication. The customs and norms that have developed in the culture of social media are more brutish than those of offline civilization. Thoughtless, uncivil behavior is far more acceptable in the virtual world than in most of the "real" communities we inhabit.

Letting it all out can feel good. That's worth something. So is engaging in civil, rational discourse. Why not use Twitter to let it out and Facebook to think it through before hitting the keyboard?

## *The Trump Phenomenon*

There is a tendency of older people to look upon the younger generations as flawed in ways "we" are not. "I had to walk barefoot two miles uphill both ways to get to school, and you're bitching about having to wait for the bus!?" I hear a lot of bitching about Millennials by Baby Boomers.

My two millennial sons and their friends have given me a fairly optimistic attitude about their generation making some needed course corrections. They are more tolerant about human relations (race, gender, orientation, etc.), more environmentally concerned, and more concerned about social justice, than their elders. Of course, they spend too much time experiencing the world through a screen and taking selfies, but they are less chauvinistic, more religiously tolerant, and less nationalistic. And, 96% of them are connected to a social media network.

Each of those observations about my sons and their millennial friends are consistent with polling data developed by the Pew Research Center. Millennials are less affiliated with organized religion and more humanistic in their values than previous generations, according to the Pew Research Center's 2014 Religious Landscape Study. So, with the demographic advance of Millennials the political future looks like a rainbow of happiness, right?

That was naive. Secularism is indeed correlated with greater tolerance of gay marriage and pot legalization. But it's also making America's partisan clashes more brutal. And it has contributed to the rise of both Donald Trump and the so-called alt-right movement, whose members see themselves as proponents of white nationalism. As Americans have left organized religion, they haven't stopped viewing politics as a struggle between "us" and "them." Many have come to define us and them in even more primal and irreconcilable ways. Peter Beinart, *The Atlantic*, "Breaking Faith: The culture war over religious morality has faded; in its place is something much worse." April 2017

The political ascendance of Donald Trump was a shock to the rosy picture of a secular-humanist-progressive world in the making. His barbaric behavior encouraged violence at some of his campaign rallies. His Twitter storms inspired rants against him and counter-rants against the ranters.

The "something worse" that Beinart fears has reared its ugly head in our current politics puts me in mind of the famous first stanza of W. B. Yeats' poem, *The Second Coming*:

Turning and turning in the widening gyre
The falcon cannot hear the falconer;
Things fall apart; the centre cannot hold;
Mere anarchy is loosed upon the world,
The blood-dimmed tide is loosed, and everywhere
The ceremony of innocence is drowned;
The best lack all conviction, while the worst
Are full of passionate intensity.

Passionate intensity in politics may be a sign of health in a democracy. But not when the passion is expressed in ad hominem attacks and violent rhetoric. It's barbaric and uncivilized.

The ancient Greeks coined the term *barbaric* to refer to anyone who didn't speak Greek. A foreign tongue sounded like "bar bar bar" sort of gibberish to the cultivated Greek ear. But calling someone a *barbarian* didn't necessarily mean that the person was uncivilized. It did mean that he was not a member of the Greek community and culture. Barbarians were "the other", foreigners within the Greek city-states who babbled in other languages and people in other lands who were not Greek. The term has evolved, so that current English usage of *barbaric* means uncivilized behavior.

The barbarism I routinely saw in political posts in social media during the 2016 presidential campaign unifies the original Greek and modern English meaning of the word. Anyone can be treated as an outsider not worthy of tolerance and civility. Although they type their messages in English, there are barbarians all around us when we enter the virtual world of social media. And we are more tempted to barbarism in that world than we are in the "real" one.

Social media lets us communicate with anyone and everyone in the common language of English. No one is excluded from the worldwide web, so long as you can get online. Because this community is so wide open the sense of connectedness within it can feel very superficial, unlike authentic communities that have grown up organically. We might gather into friend circles and private groups to create a sense of community. But online communities do not have the same sense of mutual obligation as offline communities. My online friends might send me "get well" wishes if I report that I'm sick. But they're not going to drive me to the doctor's office.

The solidarity and support of online communities is shallow. Even within those communities we are not necessarily sheltered from attack or hindered from attacking. We can behave barbarically within social media, because we can. Why restrain ourselves from incivility?

Donald Trump began his campaign for President by promising to build a wall to keep out the barbarian Mexicans, who rape and kill us. Among his first acts as President was terminating the asylum program for vetted Syrian refugees and barring Muslims from seven countries from entering the US. Courts struck down both executive orders frustrating President Trump's efforts to keep the feared hordes of barbarian refugees from crossing our borders.

In his campaign Donald Trump described a dark apocalyptic-vision of the world. America is surrounded by evil-doers intent on our destruction. But, he assured Americans that he "alone can keep us safe" by building a wall and barring the hordes of dark-skinned immigrants who want to over-run our country. The rallying cry shouted by his fans during Trump's campaign speeches was: "Build the wall!" Trump supporters were convinced that to make America great again she must become a walled fortress to keep out the barbarians. Yet, their hero's barbaric behavior and rhetoric was encouraged by their chants at his rallies and "likes" of his twitter storms.

Trump eschewed many of the traditional methods of political campaigning. He did very little fundraising during the Republican primaries. While his foes scurried from fundraiser to fundraiser raising their multi-million dollar war chests, Trump heckled them and watched his polling numbers climb. He reveled in making fun of "low energy" Jeb Bush, the early favorite to win the Republican nomination. Bush spent over $35 million in his short-lived campaign. He was slaughtered by Trump in the primaries. Clinton spent twice as much money as Trump; three times as much, if you include political action committee money. Trump outsmarted all of his opponents by getting daily free-news coverage for his bombastic style and outrageous statements.

And, he was the first major politician to use social media (Twitter) as his favorite campaign medium. Trump combined Twitter storms with old fashion rallies to charge up his followers. If you missed him on the news shows, just open your Twitter feed and you'd see a Trump tweet or a tweet about Trump trending every day during the campaign. He was disgustingly offensive or delightfully charismatic, depending on your politics and personality type.

Love him or hate him, the news media and social media users treated The Donald like the entertaining celebrity he was – either fawning over him or sniping at him. No other candidate or politician in the history of presidential campaigns garnered as much media attention as Trump did during the 2016 presidential primaries and general election.

Trump's outrageous tweets and high-testosterone rallies were appealing to a large segment of American voters. His huge personality, P. T. Barnum showmanship, and unorthodox campaign style developed a fanatical following more typical of a celebrity than a politician. The fanaticism of his followers was so intense that, as Trump bragged at a rally in Iowa, "I could stand in the middle of 5th Avenue and shoot somebody and I wouldn't lose voters."

His dark vision, jingoistic rhetoric, and arrogance infuriated Democrats, most voters who lean left, and many moderates. Trump's anti-Mexican, anti-Muslim, and anti-refugee diatribes turned most liberal Christians against him. His mocking of a disabled reporter, the video of Trump bragging to Billy Bush about sexually assaulting women, and claiming a judge was biased against him because the judge's heritage is Mexican, incensed feminists and civil rights advocates. He insulted or ridiculed, at one time or another, just about every demographic category, except white men and the elderly.

There was no way this vulgar buffoon could beat out all the other Republican candidates for the nomination. Okay, he did. But he absolutely could not beat Hillary Clinton, the nominee with the best resume of any presidential candidate since Thomas Jefferson. But he did.

The Trump strategy used the angry polarization of American voters and inflamed it. What seemed stupid or suicidal turned out to be a brilliant campaign strategy. The downside was that by exacerbating polarization during the campaign it became impossible to unite the country behind the newly elected President. Trump's "anti" remarks turned vast numbers of certain "identity groups" against him – and not mildly, but vehemently. Liberal-progressive Dems and their political allies among African-Americans, Millennials, Latinos, feminists, disabled advocates, human rights activists, etc., do not look upon Trump as a political opponent who defeated their candidate in an election. Many hate him.

We probably won't (one hopes) find out whether Trump's core supporters would vote for him again if he shot someone in the middle of 5th Avenue or not. But it's clear that Trump has attracted a loyal following that is delighted by his tweets and remarks which offend and alienate those on the other side of the political divide. That Trump pissed off the Lib-Dems, Millennials, and minorities was a huge plus in the Trump column for many of his white working-class, isolationist, anti-government, free enterprise advocates, white nationalist, and elderly supporters.

Trump's lightening-rod personality and maverick campaign-style widened the right/left divide within America even more so than the undertones of racism that the Obama presidency brought to the surface. That Hillary Clinton is a baby-boomer feminist brought out the misogyny of some voters. Her gender and feminist political stance contributed to the emotionally charged division of the electorate. It infuriated many "educated feminist-women" (Hillary supporters) that so many men and "less educated" women were willing to forgive as "locker room talk" Trump's grossly misogynistic bragging to Billy Bush in the video released by *The Washington Post* about a month before Election Day.

Yet, whatever setback his campaign suffered, Donald Trump responded with counter punches. (He has described himself as "a counter-puncher".) Instead of responding to his inflammatory speeches and tweets with meek embarrassment and calls for apologies one might have expected of his evangelical Christian supporters, they shouted, "Lock her up!" at Trump rallies and the Republican Convention. Trump encouraged his Twitter followers to refer to the first woman to be nominated for President by a major party as "Lying Hillary".

Clinton's decision to make her central campaign theme Trump's unfitness to be President just added fuel to the polarizing fire in the electorate. Hillary-haters already hated her, but her relentless attacks on their guy's character infuriated Trump supporters.

So, by the time the election was over in November family members were boycotting Thanksgiving dinners and friends were refusing to speak to each other. Private pages on Facebook limited to those who were on one side or the other of the election sprung up, so the un-like minded couldn't spoil the pity party or victory celebration.

The diameter of our silos shrank and the walls became thicker after the results of the November 8, 2016 election came in.

Is this really the culture we want to live in?

## *Devaluation of Truth as a Consequence of the Trump Phenomenon*

*Huffington Post* ran an article entitled, "Trump Reverses Himself on 6 Major Issues in 2 Days," on March 13, 2017. Past Presidents have changed their positions after they were elected often enough that it's not a shock when a President breaks a campaign pledge. H. W. Bush: "No new taxes." He raised them. W. Bush: "I'm against regime change." That's exactly what he tried to do in both Afghanistan and Iraq. But Trump's whirlwind change of positions on issues is unprecedented. Reversals on six major issues in the first two months in office – that's shocking!

Donald Trump's lack of regard for facts and evidence -- the truth – is also shocking. In an April 3, 2017 editorial the *Los Angeles Times* called the new President "the liar in chief", because of the numerous lies documented by the mainstream media. A week earlier, *Huffington Post* ran a story documenting "100 incidents of egregious falsehoods" in the first 36 days of the Trump Administration.

> All presidents lie, but lying so brazenly and so frequently about even silly factoids like his golf game has put Trump in his own category. His disregard for the truth is reflected in his top aides, who have inflated easily disproved figures like the attendance at his inauguration and even cited terror attacks that never happened.
> Igor Bobic, "The First 100 Lies: The Trump Team's Flurry of Falsehoods," Feb. 28, 2017

Because of his lack of regard for facts, evidence, and rationality, some political analysts discern in Donald Trump a figure far more sinister than just an unorthodox outsider. He's been compared by some to the irreverent and anti-elitist Andrew Jackson. But Trump's populist appeal has an element in it unlike Jackson's and other populist demagogues in American history. Trump is the first to receive information about reality, and to try to change perceptions of it, through social media. Twitter allows him a form of access to his followers that did not exist when Andrew Jackson, William Jennings Bryan, Huey Long, or any other populist representative of the white underclass ran for office. Trump has a tool at his disposal to try to shape his followers' understanding of the world more powerful than any previous populist leader.

Candidate Trump was welcomed into the informational silos of those attracted to his message of "us versus them". His divisive message encouraged a new form of siloing by his followers. Any adverse media coverage of The Donald was "fake news". Only complimentary reporting should be considered real news.

The *LA Times* Editorial Board described Trump as both Machiavellian and simple-minded in a series of editorials running daily the first week of April 2017. He is brilliant like a fox in his manipulation of the public and news media. But he comes across as a simpleton because of his lack of knowledge and his inarticulateness. The *LA Times* series of editorials blamed Trump's lack of knowledge, in part, on the narrowness of his news sources. The best evidence of his linguistic in-artfulness, the editor-authors claimed, is his tweets.

Whether Trump is feared as a dark genius and wannabe tyrant or scorned as a lucky bumbler, his critics all point to his use of Twitter to make their case. Mike Mairani posits "In Trump's Amerika," *Vanity Fair*, April 2017 that Trump is following a playbook developed by Vladimir Putin's "political technologist", Vladislav Surkov. The strategy devised by Surkov is designed to use "conflict to create a constant state of destabilized perception, in order to manage and control." In the US "Trump's team is finding ways to approximate Putin's capacity to create an alternative reality."

Mairani argues that, like Putin before him, Trump intentionally lies and distracts from the truth to create chaos and to breed cynicism, so that the public either does not know what to believe is true, or, believes that there is no truth. Trump attacks the legitimate press as "the enemy of the people". He changes positions on issues from day-to-day, but denies that he's altered his stance on any issue.

> The Oxford English Dictionary's 2016 Word of the Year was "post-truth": an adjective "relating to or denoting circumstances in which objective facts are less influential in shaping public opinion than appeals to emotion and personal belief."
> Jeanie Chung, *Tableau*, University of Chicago Division of Humanities, "The Fight for Truth," Spring 2017

Ms. Chung concludes her linguistic analysis of the term, post-truth: "Yet we seem to have created a post-truth world in which many people readily believe 'alternative facts' or 'fake news'." President Trump is a prime mover in a cultural shift which deemphasizes the value of telling the truth. A "bullshitter doesn't care about truth or falsity. The bullshitter's interest lies entirely in getting the listener to act or think in a certain way -- regardless of whether the listener's motivation is based in truth or not." *Ibid*

Chung doesn't mention Donald Trump in her piece and doesn't label the President a bullshitter. She doesn't have to. It's obvious. She does cite several sources dating back to Plato and Aristotle to make the case that a lack of regard for the truth is a danger to democracy. "The truth has always been subject to manipulation, especially by those in power." It's up to the people, the voters, to see through the manipulation.

Where Trump has even surpassed Vladimir Putin in the technique of "destabilized perception" is his use of social media, according to Mairani in his *Vanity Fair* article. "One of Trump's most effective methods for controlling the public and media discourse is his use of Twitter."

Social media is on the front lines of a cultural battle between forces that want to reclaim the traditional value of truth telling and those that profit from a post-truth culture. Americans like to think of our democratic republic as stable, eternal, and a light unto the world. No human system of government lasts forever. How ours changes should be decided by we the people while thinking clearly and objectively about where we want the country to go and what we want our country to be. We must not be bamboozled with post-truth unreality.

We need to remember that there are facts and there is truth in human reality. Our politics should have the stability of Newtonian physics. Our lived reality is not the spooky realm of relativistic sub-atomic physics. The number of people that attended the Trump inauguration is a verifiable fact within a margin of error. That fewer people attended it than the Obama inauguration is also a verifiable fact. Accurate pictures don't lie. When the new President and his press secretary claimed theirs was the largest crowd ever to witness a presidential inauguration, they lied. That first lie started the Trump White House down a path that is dangerous to democracy. It is increasingly likely that path will lead to the impeachment of President Trump.

Whether you voted for or against Trump, we all have a stake in being able to rely on our elected leaders to be honest with us. If that confidence erodes to the point that we don't care, danger lies ahead. Because we will have nothing more solid to base decisions on than unsupported beliefs and irrational emotion. That takes us to the place where Putin's Russia is now, and where other fascist and Marxist states have been. It's not a pretty place.

What can we, as citizens and social media users, do to try to avoid this fate for our country?

## *Social Media Can Be a Saving Angel (or a Tool of the Devil)*

Social media has become a tool of tyrants, demagogues, and terrorists. It's become the preferred platform for hateful and snarky attacks and counter-attacks among political foes. It is also a tool anyone can use to ferret out and spread the truth. It is the favorite tool of reformers and revolutionaries within authoritarian states. It can be used to test opposing opinions on solving political problems by rational debate and argument. It might even be used to promote a sense of unity, rather than disunity, within a nation.

So far, the evidence and arguments put forward in this book present a gloomy picture of current use and the future of social media. Narcissic blather is more common than edifying and uplifting messages; angry rants more numerous than thoughtful posts. But there are movements afoot that counter such a pessimistic forecast, at least for Facebook.

Producers of National Public Radio (NPR) became so concerned about the nation's polarization during the presidential campaign that, after the election, a one-hour nightly call-in program was created with the intention of promoting civil conversations about issues of national importance during the first 100 days of the Trump Presidency. Different hosts with different political leanings appeared on the show, called "Indivisible".

During each show the hosts and callers engaged in discussions about a range of topics, but the common theme tying the topics together was participants take on how Trump was doing within the first 100 days of his presidency. Callers were encouraged to weigh in, but to stay on topic and remain civil. Each show was immediately released as an unedited podcast. *Indivisible* was produced by WNYC, Minnesota Public Radio News, and *The Economist.* From the show's website: "Each night is a call-in. Indivisible is about being heard."

I listened to a few of the shows and was impressed by the hosts' civility toward each other when they were on opposite sides of the political divide. The hosts were also courteous with callers with whom they disagreed. The show's producers were very successful in getting calls from a wide spectrum of political perspectives.

A few callers at first sounded pretty emotional, but with polite requests by the hosts, they calmed down and made their opinions or concerns clear and without undue hostility. The callers on the shows I heard were genuinely interested in participating in a civil conversation, rather than the typical rants of AM radio shows, like Rush Limbaugh's. Making the ground rule clear, that a civil tone was expected, was key to making the shows work as a forum of serious discussion.

The *Indivisible* website also encourages listeners to tweet reactions to the discussions. This component of the show was less successful at maintaining a civil tone than the call-in portion. Many of the tweets I reviewed were civil, and all were much less toxic than the politically oriented tweets that I typically see on my own Twitter feed. Example: "#IndivisibleRadio I think that too many times we make caricatures of people whose views we oppose without really knowing them." But, some were quite angry in tone and used unnecessary CAPITALS or exclamation marks! Most of the tweets I read on the site were anti-Trump. Two examples: "#IndivisibleRadio Trump is a madman surrounded by people with no empathy who somehow think they are righteous" and "@WNYC @POTUS Yes, he's even more unfit than I thought he was three months ago. He is dangerously ill. And a traitor."

The difference in success of call-in versus Twitter, at maintaining civility and seriousness, reinforces the discussion above about the difference between virtual and offline reality. Although callers were not in the visual presence of the hosts, they were operating in real time and interacting directly with a person on the vocal level. And, they were screened by a station operator who cautioned each caller to be civil in how they expressed themselves. So, even though the tweeters were presumably aware of the show's purpose, the nature of Twitter over-rode the civility rule for many tweeters. Its 140-character limitation and the impersonality of virtual reality create such a powerful temptation toward incivility, that even on a civilized NPR discussion board some could not resist the temptation.

Another effort to address the nation's uncivil polarization is Better Angels, "a bipartisan network of leaders and organizations whose vision is to reunite America," according to the organization's website. Its founder, David Blankenhorn, is described as: "A Democrat who has for years worked to bolster family formation now seeks to call forth honest and charitable discourse with the Better Angels project." The project's mission is "To Restore Public Discourse".

When you join Better Angels (as I did), you receive this message:

> Welcome to Better Angels--you have become part of a bipartisan network of leaders and organizations committed to reducing polarization. Thank you for helping us bring people together from across the divides to rethink currently polarized issues, show why reducing polarization is an urgent priority, and advocate for

governmental and institutional reforms that will permit progress and compromise to be substituted for impasse and frustration.

We are hard at work on setting a national agenda for depolarization and will keep you informed of our progress. In the meantime, help reduce polarization by learning the 7 habits of a depolarizer.

Don't forget to tell your friends about Better Angels. Send them this link: http://better-angels.org/join/ and ask them to join. Reducing polarization in America won't happen until thousands and ultimately millions of Americans are willing to take a stand.

A "depolarizer" sounds like a ghost buster or someone who rescues brainwashed family members from cults. There is actually a parallel between depolarizing and deprogramming someone whose ability to think clearly is compromised due to brainwashing by a cult. But the deprogramming of depolarization is not what you do to someone else. It's a transformation of your own mind, which will improve the way you interact with others when you talk about politics.

Making use of them (habits of depolarization) certainly doesn't tell me what to think about any particular issue, but attending to them does seem to help me think more carefully and, I hope, more honestly. Ultimately habits of mind oriented to depolarization are, to change metaphors again, less a microscope than a new pair of glasses -- less a way of seeing a few things more clearly than a different way of seeing many things. And surely a different way of seeing is what's needed. As Lincoln put it in 1862, "when the occasion is piled high with difficulty, the first and great challenge is to think anew."
David Blankenhorn, *The American Interest*, "The Seven Habits of Highly Depolarizing People," Feb. 15, 2016

What Blankenhorn is advocating in his "7 habits of depolarization" is to become an empathetic listener and clear, rational, and respectful speaker. The transformation he is calling for is not so much a technique to change other people as a way to transform your self. His hope is that, if enough selves are changed, America will be transformed out of its current toxic polarity into a more unified country. Blankenhorn wants to use Better Angels to put the unum back in e pluribus unum. He's not advocating a Nazi-like unity of robots that always agree with each other. He just wants to promote unity as in a commitment of citizens to converse respectfully with each other about political issues.

Better Angels is promoting depolarization through a multi-faceted approach combining the retail one-to-one and a systemic strategy. It is publishing articles and seeking publicity in the mass media. It puts out podcasts, and has even done a cross-country bus tour. It's also on Facebook and Twitter. The Better Angels posts I've seen in social media are instructional rather than actual engagements of citizens in the kind of dialogue Blankenhorn recommends.

The primary putsch of Better Angels is to hold workshops in which people of opposing political views practice engaging in civil conversations. Results of a workshop held in Waynesville, Ohio, with "fifteen area residents who had participated -- seven conservative-leaning and pro-Trump and eight liberal-leaning and anti-Trump" was summarized in the Better Angels eLetter of May 9, 2017 as follows:

> We found that we are less different from one another, and less hostile to one another, than the pundits in the media typically say we are. A number of us on both sides began our meeting believing that the other side could not be dealt with on the basis of rational thought. We say unanimously that our experience of talking with, rather than at or about, each other caused us to abandon that belief. We say unanimously that real people are more complicated and appealing than the stereotypes we have of them.
>
> In this meeting, we did not change our views on issues. But we did change our views of each other. And surely, in this time of extreme public rancor and mistrust, this change is a good thing for us and for the land we all love.

On its Facebook page there are posts with tips on how to engage in civil discourse and links to articles about it. The same is true about the Better Angels' tweets on its Twitter page. I suspect that the Better Angels social media managers did not think Twitter or Facebook could work as forums for civil engagement by political adversaries.

I didn't want to speculate. I wanted to try it out on my Facebook page to find out.

# VI. The Experiment Worked (sort of)

*There are two ways of acquiring knowledge, one through reason, the other by experiment. Argument reaches a conclusion and compels us to admit it, but it neither makes us certain nor so annihilates doubt that the mind rests calm in the intuition of truth, unless it finds this certitude by way of experience. Thus many have arguments toward attainable facts, but because they have not experienced them, they overlook them and neither avoid a harmful nor follow a beneficial course. Even if a man that has never seen fire, proves by good reasoning that fire burns, and devours and destroys things, nevertheless the mind of one hearing his arguments would never be convinced, nor would he avoid fire until he puts his hand or some combustible thing into it in order to prove by experiment what the argument taught. But after the fact of combustion is experienced, the mind is satisfied and lies calm in the certainty of truth. Hence argument is not enough, but experience is.*

Roger Bacon, ***On Experimental Science***, 1268

## *Introduction of the Experiment on Facebook*

I was ready for resistance. And some anti-Trump friends made it very clear they saw no value in trying to engage in conversations on Facebook or anywhere with Trump supporters. The response of one friend to my invitation to participate in the experiment: "Sorry, people. And by people I mean H_, Jeff Rasley, and others of you giving dialogue a valiant try. I can't. I just can't. This is my line in the sand."

Other friends signaled they were willing to try. So I began the experiment with this FB post:

> February 24, 2017 at 5:00pm • I'm going to try using Facebook and Twitter differently. The experiment might fail, but it's worth a try. ... "Liberals" fear the loss of freedom in the form of human rights through authoritarian use of government. "Conservatives" fear the loss of freedom in the form of personal security through bureaucratic-governmental control. Can we find common ground for breaking out of these separate silos by recognizing we all want personal freedom of expression and personal security? Extremists at each end of the political spectrum may be unable to respect alternative views. The rest of us should be flexible and tolerant enough to listen and respond respectfully.

I embedded images of the dove of peace and a raised fist in the post.

22 different friends commented. Several comments generated numerous replies. Sub-threads developed with ten or more participants jumping into these side-conversations. 29 friends "liked" the post.

I was satisfied with the response in terms of the interest it generated. But my fear that anti-Trump friends might refuse to participate was justified, it seemed. Many friends posted comments indicating they were unsympathetic to the idea of engaging in respectful dialogue across ideological lines. The friends that were the most critical of engaging in cross-ideological lines are all self-identified anti-Trump voters and liberal progressives or socialists. The concern expressed in my post, "Extremists at each end of the political spectrum may be unable to respect alternative views," was predictive.

A sampling of the comments critical of the project:

Shortly after the election I made the decision to become one the people you are demonizing here. It was a conscious decision to no longer be nice and unobjectionable. I have become ruthless, vulgar and in-your-face. Being passive may earn you friends, but it gets you nowhere politically. The one thing I am careful to still do, however, is provide solid sources to back up my claims. That's something that - in my personal experience - the far right can't (or isn't willing) to do.

You ask does the other side have the right to hold an opposing view. Sure as long as they don't act on it. But elections have consequences. Elections kill people. ... Sorry, Jeff. I'm not with you on this one.

I would no more be willing to listen to a Trump supporters views than with Sadam Hussein's. What is the outcome you are looking for? I can't image what benefit it would bring either of us.

Trump supporters embrace white supremacy, they think grabbing women by the pussy is "no big deal", they call people of color "nigg**s". No sorry, unacceptable!!! Do you want to understand their rationale??? There is none.

Jeff - Here's how these types of conversations have gone for me in the past ... Me: Where do you get your news from then? Other: Fox News, the Conservative Daily, Righter than Right, etc. Me: You're fucking stupid. (Unfriend) LOL

Resistance to the Trump administration was translated by these left-leaning friends of mine into resistance to communicating with Trump supporters. The hostility was understandable. Their side lost the 2016 Presidential Election and is in the minority in Congress. I suspect they would have been more open to dialogue with the other side had Clinton won. Anti-Obama friends might have opposed the proposal had it been suggested after his election. But the shoe was on the other foot now. No pro-Trump friends expressed opposition to the project.

An analysis of the responses indicated that respondents skewed about one-third pro-Trump and two-thirds anti-Trump. That disparity may be an indicator of my own unintended siloing. Even though I was not a rabid anti-Trump poster on Facebook, I did indicate my opposition in various ways.

There were pro and anti Trump friends in favor of the project. A sampling of their initial comments:

I agree. I think we should be able to understand where the other person is coming from and why they have the views that they do. Instead of instantly hating each other for having separate beliefs try to find understanding in what we believe and why we believe it.

I agree with Jeff. The more centrist members of all parties have got to start talking rationally!

If we treat each other as equal, dignified human beings, place ideology to the side, and listen attentively with our hearts your suggestions are very possible.

Yours is a great and noble idea.

Since the majority of responses to the initial post were either critical or skeptical of the idea, I tried rephrasing the project as:

Feb 25, 2017 Jeff Rasley at 12:09pm. What I would like to do is to use this space as a place where opposing/differing views are expressed and responded to with interest and respect, not with anger or ridicule. There are many places where only one point of view is welcome. Have we become so divided, and so sure that "we" are right and "they" are wrong, that we are unable to listen and try to understand "the other side"? Can we express our own point of view without trying to persuade others that ours is the only worthy position?

This post received 25 "likes", four less than the original, and far fewer responses. A couple of the responses to the second post were skeptical it would work, but no one expressly criticized it. A few were positive, and one friend was enthusiastically supportive. She commented, "Love love love this!!!!!!"

## *Facilitating Civil Conversations about "Hot" Political Issues on Facebook*

Over the next few weeks I introduced a series of controversial issues on my FB page and asked friends to respond. Interestingly, none of the particular issues generated as much antagonism in the comments as the initial question about whether friends would be willing to engage in discussion threads with people on the other side of the political divide. Equally interesting, all of the friends, except one, who were sharply critical of the project, did participate in the follow-up posts on specific issues. The friend who notified me that she would not participate before I began the experiment ("I just can't. This is my line in the sand.") turned out to be one of the most active participants. So did the friend who responded to the initial post with, "Sorry Jeff, I'm not with you on this one."

The initial reaction of many of the angry Liberal Progressives was an impulsive, Hell no! I don't want to talk to those blankety-blank Trump supporters. When they gave it more thought, all but one of the critics were willing to give it a try.

The first topic introduced was immigration reform. My post was:

Feb 26, 2017 Jeff Rasley at 12:00pm •
Immigration. Seems to me that immigration policy in a modern nation-state must balance national security with the values obtained from tourism/travel, supply of needed workers and entrepreneurs, and providing refuge to political dissenters and others fleeing persecution. So, the policy would have 2 major objectives: 1. Barring entry to anyone for whom there is reason to suspect of violent or criminal intent; 2. Admitting all others to the extent the economy can support it and/or is benefited. This balance doesn't seem like it would be impossible to express in laws & regulations, but our US Congress, the EU, and political parties seem to have failed to do so. Most everyone agrees the current situation in both Europe & the US is unsatisfactory. What's the solution?

The post only generated comments from six friends. That was disappointing. It seemed that my FB friends were less interested in addressing specific issues than expressing their opinions on whether dialogue between political opponents was worthwhile. So, I followed up the post on immigration with a post pointing out the reduction in responses and asking friends what they thought that meant.

> February 27 at 8:27pm • In response to my last post about immigration, each of the posts by friends in that thread was a thoughtful expression of rational discourse on a divisive political issue. But note how many- many more posts were written in response to my first question about whether we can engage on FB in a tolerant & respectful manner about divisive political issues. Social media is so often a silo where only similar views are expressed. Or, people with opposing views shout at, insult, and ridicule each other. What does it say about our culture that so many of us either prefer not to communicate with people of opposing views or we just want to attack & insult?

(I included an image that I thought might help draw attention to each post during the experiment. This image went with that post.)

The post only garnered a few responses, but it might have inspired more responses to the next issue-oriented post. Or, maybe friends were just more interested in expressing themselves about ISIS than immigration. How the US should respond to ISIS is, I think, as complex a question as how to reform immigration policy. But our antennae have been so sensitized to terrorism as a hot topic, everyone has an opinion on it. My guess is that, unless you are directly affected by it, an opinion on immigration reform is more difficult to develop and articulate. ISIS as a topic probably inspires more impulsive responses, so it's ready made for social media users. I introduced the topic with this post:

> Jeff Rasley March 1 at 12:02pm • Continuing my effort to offer a forum for rational discourse about controversial topics, I'd like to consider ISIS. Last night Pres. Trump stated that there was a plan in place to "extinguish" ISIS "from the planet." Does the US have a national interest in destroying ISIS? If so, what cost in casualties and resources is that goal worth?

This generated 29 comments and multiple replies to some of the comments. Several of the comments were quite emotional, and the ground rule of civility was pushed to the limits by a couple respondents. I was even accused of being 'rude" by a friend with whom I exchanged comments. I apologized, but explained I was trying to be sarcastic, not rude. She accepted, and we got back on topic.

The least civil comment was: "Trump is that group's (ISIS) wet dream for recruiting purposes. His blather confirms the propaganda they peddle." Although it uses kind of inflammatory language, the comment makes an important point for consideration: that anti-Muslim rhetoric by our leaders helps ISIS, rather than hurts it. And, the commenter did not personally attack any other commenter. So, it was within the bounds of the ground rules of the project.

Many of the comments within the ISIS discussion-thread were thoughtful and incisive about the complex issue of defeating violent radicalism. Various strategies and tactics were proposed. On the stark issue of whether the US should engage in all-out war against ISIS or not, three general positions were staked out: 1. Yes, defeat them militarily, 2. Engage in limited combat operations, and support local parties fighting ISIS (i.e., maintain the status quo), and 3. Stay out of it. No anti-Trump friends lined up under #1; they were split between #2 and #3. Only pro-Trump friends supported #1, but not uniformly. Two expressed doubt about the effectiveness of a purely military solution and supported the isolationist position of #3. That's where some leftists and right-wingers found common ground -- opposing further military intervention in the Mideast.

The conversation progressed so productively it diverged into the issue of whether humanity is becoming more or less violent. I tried to sum up the discussion with this comment:

The responses to the question have been really interesting (at least to me), and almost entirely respectful of differing views. A well-researched and interesting book that makes this case: "Believe it or not, today we may be living in the most peaceful moment in our species' existence." Pinker's historical optimism describes ISIS as an outlier, which will be defeated. How and when remains to be seen and I would prefer my son's life not be put at risk to do so. I'd like to see the US follow a middle course of vigorously supporting the local forces that have been directly attacked by ISIS, but commit very limited ground troops of our own. And, I think we should cooperate with the Russians & Syrian government to defeat ISIS. Assad can be dealt with later. I don't think solving the Syrian civil war should be the US's obligation. And, I agree with the other commentators who have made the point that military alone cannot defeat violent radicalism. Showing our country and culture to offer a better life than extremist ideologies is a long-term and complicated effort.

The next topic was narrower and more immediate:

Jeff Rasley at 12:00pm • I'd like to continue our experiment with trying to engage in civil conversation about controversial political topics with a very specific and current one: Should Jeff Sessions resign as US Attorney General? Why or why not? It seems clear that he did have contact with the Russian ambassador to the US during the presidential campaign, and he was not accurate in his response to questions about contact with Russians during his confirmation hearing. But is that so significant that he should not serve as US AG?

28 friends participated in this discussion. Only three defended Sessions, and thought he should be confirmed as US Attorney General. The other commenters thought he should either resign or be fired. Several respondents wanted Sessions to be prosecuted for perjury.

Rational evidence-based arguments were made on both sides, but the thread developed primarily into one pro-Trump defender of Sessions responding to the many anti-Trump commenters arguing that Sessions should not be able to serve as the US AG. A sampling of the comments:

As I posted, even the minimally pejorative interpretation of the Attorney General's conduct raises grave doubts about his suitability for a post that requires great discretion. He has been, at the very least, less than candid responding to questions under oath. He either has not consumed or has not adopted the unanimous conclusion of US intelligence agencies that Russia meddled in our election. He is puzzled why people care about these things. Inattention and indifference are not qualities we seek in our top law enforcement official.

Yeah, like Obama's AG having a private meeting with Bill Clinton just before she makes a decision to bring charges against Hillary, should be an AG. Give me a break!!! Jeff Sessions met with a Russian ambassador strictly as a Senator, as they might do, as part of their job. Sessions at the time was absolutely no part of a Trump campaign. And BTW, it wouldn't matter whether Sessions did or didn't have contact with a Russian Ambassador, it's totally immaterial. Jeff should stay the course.

Sorry, Jeff Sessions was involved with the Trump campaign at the time of his meeting with Russian ambassador. Sessions was one of Trump campaign advisor. Maybe this would have been considered an oversight on Sessions' part, if the Republicans had not made such an overreaction to Hillary's behavior. People in glass houses should not throw stones. It may be like a boomerang!

Russia had absolutely no bearing on what the outcome of our election was. Hillary lost on her own with no help from anyone else. People need to get that thru their thick skulls. Enough is enough.

I have it through my thick skull that Trump won. "Russia had absolutely no bearing on what the outcome of our election was"? Maybe. Maybe not. It is clear, though, that Russia tried to have a bearing on our election, and the means it used are worth understanding, even if there were no effect this time, and that's true whether the Trump campaign was tied to the efforts or not. The public evidence, alone, of Trump campaign ties to Russian operative and of the Trump economic empire's connections with Russia require, at least, more transparency. There is more here than the question of whether Trump won the election.

The two sides of the argument were staked out as pro and anti Trump. There was no cross over. It was a totally partisan debate. Except, one pro-Trump friend, near the end of the thread indicated that she was wavering in her support of Sessions, because of what she learned from the anti-Sessions posts.

The discussion veered off into comparing Bill Clinton's lies with Sessions' untruths. The primary Sessions defender accused the Sessions prosecutors of hypocrisy, because (he assumed) they didn't think President Clinton should have been forced to resign or to be criminally charged for his lies about sex with Monica Lewinsky and other women. The defense to the charge of hypocrisy was one of "false equivalency". An example of the response to the charge of hypocrisy by an anti-Sessions friend was:

> In that case the "lie" had an excuse like this one. What Clinton claimed was that what they did was not in his view "sex". Now, we may find this bit of language ridiculous, but let's look at the difference here: 1. A man lies about cheating on his wife or 2. A man was secretly meeting with Russian officials (which no other senators in the committee did during the election), and there is currently an investigation about how our president may be connected to Russia in a lot of unsavory ways. Yes, both are bad. One endangers our entire electoral system; the other is a terrible husband who may not have much respect for Congress.

There was real flair to the discussion. There were quite a few one-sentence responses, just indicating the friend's position, pro or con, but many comments were thoughtful articulate arguments. Historical examples were raised. Information and opinions about the extent of Russian interference in the presidential election were exchanged. The primary pro-Sessions participant provided a definition of "impeachment", along with a history lesson about President Clinton's impeachment.

> Yes, William Jefferson Clinton was impeached. Chief Prosecutor, David Schippers, and his team reviewed the material and determined there was sufficient evidence to impeach the president. As a result, four charges were considered by the full House of Representatives; two passed (Perjury and Obstruction of justice), making Clinton the second president to be impeached. For removal from office, 67 Senate votes were needed, 50 votes on Perjury were cast for removal

and 45 on Obstruction of Justice. No Democrats voted for removal on either charge, acquitting Clinton (no removal of office). You may have considered Clinton to be a Southern Gentleman, but I'll bet the women who were sexually assaulted and abused by him (while governor of Alabama) didn't feel the same way. Clinton was the second President to be impeached. Clinton was impeached on December 19, 1998.

But the thread veered back to the narrow issue with arguments, like the following, eventually overwhelming in quantity the, by then, lone defender of Sessions.

Clinton's case was altogether different because his lie occurred in a deposition in private litigation completely unrelated to national policy, did not involve allegedly unlawful conduct but rather just sex between consenting adults (which happens frequently, by the way) and it wasn't his job to run an agency that was tasked with investigating it. And the lying under oath there was not in order to get the job of President in the first place.

Friends did not want to let this discussion end. I had to twice signal an ending. Even after the second attempt, a few more comments were posted. This was how I first tried to bring the thread to a close:

Thanks to all for posting civilly on a controversial topic. I'd like to wrap up this thread and move on to another -- US relations with Russia. See the next post. I especially want to thank P___ for his posts, because he expressed a minority view (at least in this thread) without much support from political allies. There does seem to be wide agreement that Sessions should, as he did, recuse himself from any relevant investigation. And, the weight of public opinion seems to be that he was not truthful in his testimony, and so his effectiveness as the AG is compromised. Whether this results in his resignation and any other legal consequences is yet to be determined.

### The Experiment Was Working, but There Was an Imbalance

I was disappointed that more pro-Trump friends did not participate. P_ valiantly defended Sessions. But he was encircled like a sheep

surrounded by wolves. The other pro-Trumpers who commented lent
minimal support, just liking or leaving one sentence affirmations of P_'s
comments. So, I messaged a friend known for his sharp intellect and severe
conservatism. I asked why he was not participating in the project.

His private reply:

Jeff, I really do appreciate your good intentions but, unfortunately my
experience with political related posts are not good.  Hopefully this
doesn't come across as pretentious, but my view is that the issue is far
greater than difference of opinion. Of course there are exceptions to
the following rule, but I find it is very much the rule. What you call
"intelligent conservatives" have essentially a Lockean view of the world-
that man is fallible and utopias are not possible. Therefore, there is
no perfect solution; you simply look for the best possible outcome.
This worldview approaches a debate as being between right and
wrong- the objective is to persuade the other side to change its mind.
Unfortunately, most of the left are Rousseauean in perspective. They
believe in their utopias and view debate as being a battle between
good and evil. And the objective is virtue signaling and the destruction
of evil. Their politics is taken on faith, like a religion without God. It's
no coincidence that a small number of my leftist friends, amongst my
300+ total facebook friends account for the actual majority of postings
on my facebook feed almost every day as they spam with every
possible article they can find that supports their views. They are
evangelizing.  I don't have any conservative friends who spam like this.
And, too often when I have entered into debates on faceback my
arguments, which I try to keep fact based and rational, are all too
often responded to with invective and name calling.  Quite frankly,
while I have a thick skin, I'm tired of being called a racist, a fascist or
whatever by someone who has never had an original much less an
intelligent thought in his life. Or being unfriended by assholes like
___. I'm sure you will disagree but I do think the left, especially the
social justice warriors, now "own" social media the way they own mass
media and the entertainment industry. I've noticed that most
"intelligent conservatives" I know have moved away from posting
anything political themselves and are much less likely to enter into a
debate thread than they used to. Me, I do occasionally still pick my
fights so you may see me respond now and then because I know your
intentions are good, but the reality is that my use of social media these

days is overwhelmingly, um, social... family events, treks, runs, my dogs, etc.

I understood his feelings. His response epitomized what I wanted to try to change about Facebook. He'd been shunned and attacked for expressing conservative views on FB.

I was sorry he was not participating in the experiment, because his participation would have helped to provide a better balance to the discussions. (Eventually he was coaxed into posting several long and detailed comments in a post-experiment thread about climate change and the Paris Accord.) Still, the experiment seemed to be working. Friends with different perspectives were engaging in political conversations on my page, and the tone had remained largely civil and respectful.

Participants were so engaged with the issue of whether Jeff Sessions should be able to serve as US Attorney General several comments were posted after I declared the thread at an end. So, I made a second attempt to wrap up the discussion with this post:

I appreciate all these additional replies. Because they do reflect that FB can be used to discuss controversial issues in which people with different/opposing views and political affiliations can participate civilly. This is exactly what I wanted to see -- whether we could leave the silos of "like mindedness" to engage with "opponents" without insult & ridicule. Thanks and see the next post about Russia & US relations.

A few friends just couldn't help themselves and still added a few more comments. P_ felt the need to demand that the commenting cease. I think he was exhausted from taking on all the anti-Trumpers.

I began the next conversation with this post:

Continuing with the effort to engage with controversial topics with reason & respect -- How should the US and Russian relations be affected, if at all, by the allegations, and evidence, that Russia engaged in activities intended to influence the Presidential Election? Isn't there a long history of US politicians and foreign governments trying to help each other in secretive ways to achieve mutually beneficial goals? E.g., Founding Fathers & France; The Brits & Confederate leaders; the Brits & Germans each aiding sympathetic US candidates leading up to and during WWI; the Brits & Germans again during WWII. Have

the Russians and the Trump campaign exceeded historical norms?
Bad thing if they did, but wouldn't it be a good thing for the US and
Russia to have better relations?

This topic only attracted nine participants into a discussion. But, in
some ways the comments were the most interesting. Those expressing
concern about Russia meddling in other nation's elections were all anti-
Trump. They articulated an understanding and concern about the
precariousness of relationships among Russia, the US, and our European
allies. They worried that Putin's and Trump's seemingly warm personal
relationship was evidence of subterranean nefariousness. They worried that
a Trump-led detente with Russia boded ill for relations within the NATO
alliance. Two examples:

> I see it as a positive when two nuclear armed super powers have better
> relations, and no doubt there is a long history of foreign attempts at
> influencing US policies. Hacking into a presidential candidates emails
> and releasing these to the public is a new development. The question
> for me is what is Trump's goal with his initiative to Russia. Is it a
> dislike of the EU approach to immigration and terrorism, an
> admiration of Putin's approach to terrorism, or is it a genuine interest
> in promoting world peace through de-escalation. Of course the other
> question is why are Trump's people lying about their Russian
> contacts. This only breeds more nefarious explanations about what is
> being hidden.

> Russia and the United States are not the only nations involved in this
> is the main thing I want to emphasize. They are not even the only
> nuclear armed nations involved. Sweden has re-introduced the draft,
> Poland is apparently feeling threatened. These nations are not
> capable of standing against the Russians by themselves and if they start
> feeling they can no longer count on the USA to stand with them
> against Russia it WILL have consequences. What will a small nation
> like Sweden do? Withdraw from the NPT since they can no longer
> count on other nuclear powers to protect them and restart their
> nuclear arms program? Change from the USA's sphere of influence
> to Russia's sphere of influence? Anyway, if they can't count on the
> USA they will need to make difficult decisions and the USA won't be
> in a position to influence those decisions.

Pro-Trump commenters were not concerned that Putin and Trump might be engaged in a conspiracy to destabilize NATO. They welcomed warmer relations with Russia. Accusations that Trump and his crew were in league with the Ruskies, and were lying about it, were dismissed as poor sportsmanship by disappointed Hillary supporters.

All this reporting about how Russia is influencing and meddling in the US affairs and everyone else's, but in Russia they are claiming that we are doing the same. And we probably are and always have been. But it's a big deal this year because a Political Party lost the election and it's trying to blame everything and everyone on their failure. Let's get over all of this, and start to mend together or the future for our Children, Grandchildren, Servicemen and women, and our Country will surely be weakened. We will be destroyed from within instead of from an outside force.

Another friend picked up on the notion that America is being destroyed from within by supporters of Obama and Hillary.

I believe that is the agenda of some to destroy from within. That is why some are encouraging and funding a lot of the protests. I could be wrong but I believe the Obama administration and if would have be elected Hillary to continue the agenda to destroy within. I can realize the agenda for Obama, he has ties to other believes and religions but Hillary is another story. I believe it was money, promised money and power that she seeked at the price of freedom for the US. This is just my take on the situation.

She added a follow-up comment excusing Trump and amplifying her accusation that, whatever Trump's faults, Hillary's are worse.

Yes it would be better for Russia and US to have better relations. Seems as though the focus is on Trump and Russia's connections with little being said about Hillary's connections and her campaign donations from other countries that are not the type to just donate money without receiving nothing in return. My understanding is that Trump primarily ran his campaign with own funds. I would also like to add that evens though Trump may not be the most educated and professional speaker and can be a little dramatic that Hillary showed her true colors by callings individuals, US citizens, names such as deplorables. Sorry to get off topic. Please correct me if I'm wrong.

It was interesting to see right there on my Facebook page the transformation in attitude of the right and left to Russia. Since the Russian Revolution in 1917 the political left in the US has been much more interested in friendship with Russia (formerly the USSR) than the right. Until Trump, the right has been hawkish and distrustful of Russia. Putin and Trump have reversed the dynamic. Now, the right is in favor of warmer relations with, and reducing or dropping sanctions against, Russia. The left is extremely distrustful of Putin and supports even more sanctions.

A surprising development was that an anti-Trump friend deleted his comment and left this paranoid-sounding explanation:

> Jeff, I periodically delete nearly all of my posts, likes, etc from FB, because especially in the Trump era I don't want to have a permanent record of all my political activities and opinions that can be subpoenaed or whatever. (Just recently Trump's administration has taken to subpoenaing social network info for people arrested protesting the Dakota pipeline and people entering the country, for example.) My only intended audience on FB is friends who are following me more or less in the moment.

Another surprise was that a friend who had not participated in the discussions, beyond "liking" the original post, unfriended me with this rather charming explanation:

> Jeff, I am contacting you to let you know I've truely enjoyed your posts. That being said, I am regrettably unfriending you in order to create a more intimate wall. Best wishes to you. Keep on traveling!

Nevertheless, I decided that the experiment had worked. The results were mixed in some respects. The number of responses on the "immigration reform" and "relations with Russia" topics was disappointing. But, the overall participation was as high, and much more in depth, than responses to my typical FB posts about family matters, social events, and travels. My garden variety FB posts would typically receive about 30 likes and 10 to 20 one-line comments. Those sorts of posts never developed so many sub-threads and replies to replies as the experimental political posts did.

The evidence was strong enough to support the case that civil discourse between those with opposing political views is possible on Facebook. To conclude the experiment, I wanted to throw out what may be the most emotionally charged political issue of modern times.

March 11 at 12:02pm • I would like to end this experiment with attempting civil conversation on FB with an issue that has bitterly divided the US for decades and which never seems to be finally resolved -- Abortion. What do you think the Trump administration should do (or not do), and what do you expect it to do (or not do) as to "women's right to choose" and "the right to life"? Thanks to all for participating!

www.shutterstock.com · 322862513

If any topic would push friends over the edge of civility, I thought "abortion" would do it. It didn't. The comments were civil. Extreme positions were taken, but opponents did not personally attack each other. What did surprise me was that several pro-Trump friends posted pro-choice comments. Only one anti-Trump friend took a strong pro-life stance within the discussion. A sampling of the comments from the Abortion thread:

The other topics were easy. You really want to open this one?

I believe in a womans right to decide what to do about her own body. Im not pro abortion, but i think you should have the freedom to choose. Even you make abortion illegal, it is not going to stop it. It will stop the safety of it. (pro-Trump friend)

I do think that a woman should never be forced to have a baby she doesn't want. On the other hand, when she is pregnant there is no longer one body, but two. And to me one is just as precious as the other! I understand that it is a huge dilemma! But foremost, a woman should try as much as possible to chose to not get pregnant! Having said that I don't believe an abortion should be denied. I believe that science will solve that problem. Perhaps in the future a procedure can be performed so that a woman cannot get pregnant and easily reversed on demand. This way there would never be an accident as it would be compulsory to have the procedure! (pro-Trump friend)

A fetus is not a human being in my opinion and if the anti-abortion crowd really is trying to save "life" they should be SCREAMING to end the Death Penalty (a barbarous practice!). The issue is also being used as a hammer to try to destroy Planned Parenthood.

Part of the problem is that, when republicans (the farther right the better) say that they are "pro-life" what they really mean is that they are "pro-birth". They certainly do not want to do anything to help nurture and raise that child.

I think the father needs a "right" too. It takes 2 to make a baby. It should take 2 to decide (yes providing the father has not ducked out of the picture). (pro-Trump friend)

Always wondered why abortion is a political issue in the States. It's not (or rather, it shouldn't be). It's the most intimate decision and it's so circumstantial. For me, the government should support its citizens' (women's) needs whatever they are, rather than impose one size fits all policies.

I don't believe Trump will try to do anything about abortion rights, but other things get lumped in with that, such as Planned Parenthood. So if your pro-choice but against Planned Parenthood, I think you're screwed. The Government makes it that way. So, I believe the ways of the Government should be stopped, not a woman's right to chose. I also do not believe that the Father has the right to chose ' for the woman '. One should not be able to force a woman to have or not have abortion as an option. However, I have never believed in helping young girls in school or unmarried prior to the age of 18 in recieving birth control. I'm sorry, it just sets the stage for behavior. And is not always going to be 100 % affective for various reasons. (pro-Trump friend)

Think back on all the kids we went to school with...how many of them didn't have sex because they were taught that it was a sin outside of marriage? How many of them got pregnant and were stigmatized into early marriages that failed? How many of them were sent off to "Homes for Unwed Mothers?" to have their babies secretly and then forced to give them up? Society made young women feel shame for the same thing it praised men for doing, and its nonsense. Men could and did do what they wanted, but if a woman was pregnant outside of marriage she bore the brunt of society's judgment. This kind of thinking makes my blood boil... How can birth control hurt anyone? Denying a woman birth control is a way for men to control them, or attempt to control them. Keep your laws off of my body, please.

I can only think of one other situation where someone feels they have the right to have say over another's body and that is slavery. It is an individual's body and she should have control over what she chooses to do with it.

I find it difficult to compare a baby's right to a life to a person on death row, but then again I don't believe in the death penalty either. Of course I wish abortion wasn't an option, but more than that, I wish everyone's eyes would be opened to what exactly goes on in an abortion. Also, that people research Margaret Sanger and all of her ideas that were the driving force to the beginning of Planned Parenthood. Wondering also, when do people who don't believe it is a baby, admit it is a baby? At four weeks? Eight weeks? Check out what a baby has developed by four weeks! (pro-Trump friend)

The most interesting thing to me is your use of the word "believe" What people do or don't believe...that seems to be the crux of part of this problem...it can't be about "beliefs" when it comes to laws, because that is too large a variable... You are free to believe as you choose, and everyone else has the same rights. There isn't any evidence that a fetus before say, 12 weeks has any kind of cognitive ability, its still developing cells. No one really knows for sure when a baby becomes a conscious being but if we can set that aside, isn't the real issue here being told by the government what you can do or not do with your body? Laws never stopped desperate women from getting abortions. Even Barbara Bush said it shouldn't be a legal question.

Original question was what did we think President Trump will do about this issue. In all probability nothing. I am personally pro life. I can't quite understand why a woman has a right to her body and the unborn child doesn't. My eldest son saw a film in the public high school in his life studies course called "The Silent Scream". He came home at 16 and cried for the baby that was killed. BTW there were 4 days dedicated to pro choice and 1 to pro life. I was one of those girls that became pregnant at 16, had my baby and kept him. I would not trade a minute of my life for what I supposedly lost due to teen pregnancy. Now death penalty is a totally different issue. Honestly feel it is appropriate in cases of heinous crimes. Mass murders, serial murders, rape of anyone (man, woman or child), hate crimes just to name a few. (anti-Trump friend)

After 20 different friends had commented (several commented or replied to other comments more than once) within the Abortion thread, I offered a compromise solution to see how it would be received. I wondered if there is any room for compromise between the pro-life and pro-choice camps.

Jeff Rasley. I want to say that I am really pleased (and a little surprised) that we've been able to have this civil discussion on such an emotionally charged issue without insults & ridicule. I think G_ makes an especially important point; if the issue is to be resolved by "belief" there is no resolution, because the 2 dominant beliefs are in direct opposition. But we can look to science for a compromise solution. When is a fetus actually viable without extraordinary support? Could both sides compromise to accept that before that line is reached abortion should be allowed on demand, but after only under extreme circumstances? As to what the Trump admin will do, it's pretty clear that abortion is not a significant issue to DJT, as he was for it, but turned against it when seeking "Evangelical" votes. However, Pence is strongly anti-abortion, and I would expect him to push for every possible restriction the government can impose within the law, e.g., de-fund Planned Parenthood.

My proposed compromise was not embraced by either camp. A sample of responses:

Thanks for the nice insights, I honestly think this is one of those without gray area...Women should not be subjected to this kind of scrutiny (i.e. when could it be acceptable to make a case for the procedure.) We should not have to talk to anyone about something this personal except the people we choose. As long as the Christian right in our country ignore science we are in trouble because they won't compromise on their beliefs. And I guess none of us should have to compromise on our beliefs, so....until we can change the conversation to one that isn't about what we believe but what we know there isn't a lot of hope.

I just want to point out that Trump is not "doing nothing." He already nominated someone to the Supreme Court who appears to align with the anti-abortion advocates (I do not use or like the term "pro-life" because it implies that if you believe that abortion should be a legal option that you are "anti-life" and I believe those two things should not be conflated). And in regards to defunding of Planned Parenthood...bills and laws have already been introduced in Congress, and he has done nothing --- which is something: tacit consent.

Conception/life begins when the sperm hits the egg. That's all I have to say about that. (pro-Trump friend)

Let women do what they wish with their own bodies, please.

A clear majority of the commenters favored allowing women to have an abortion, if they chose to. This is consistent with opinion polls. But the results in my experiment were even more pro-choice than nationwide opinion polls. The Pew Research Center summarizes its findings as follows: "As of 2016, public support for legal abortion is as high as it has been in two decades of polling. Currently, 57% say abortion should be legal in all or most cases, while 39% say it should be illegal in all or most cases." (January 11, 2017) The ratio of my respondents was about 75% pro choice and 25% pro life.

### Conclusion of the Experiment

No consensus developed around a compromise position on abortion. But that was how each of the threads went. Friends on different sides of each issue expressed their views and disagreements. Point/counterpoint arguments turned into sub-threads as replies to particular comments and replies to replies. A few participants did indicate they would continue thinking about points made in a particular thread when signing off from a discussion. Two commenters expressed uncertainty about where they stood on an issue, after participating in a discussion. No one admitted that they were persuaded to abandon a position stated at the beginning of the discussion in favor of another by the end of the thread. No winners or loser were declared.

That was not the point or my expectation.

The purpose was to try to find out whether FB friends with opposing political views could engage in civil discourse with each other about political issues. Would they be able to attack the arguments of the other side, and even pillory Trump and Hillary, but refrain from insulting each other? Yes, for the most part the participants remained civil to each other.

A few friends only contributed one-line responses. A few just sniped at those on the other side of the political divide. However, it was clear that many of the participants thought through the issues raised, marshaled evidence to support their position, and then laid out their argument. It was also clear that many of those who jumped into the point/counterpoint sub-threads thought about what others posted and crafted replies to counter the arguments in dispute. There were a few arguments about relevant facts, but most of the arguments that developed in the sub-threads were over how to interpret, or what to do about, the facts relevant to the situation.

For example, in the Jeff Sessions thread there was general agreement that Sessions was not completely truthful during his confirmation hearing in his response to the question about contacts with Russian officials. A debate developed over whether his lack of candor should disqualify him from serving as US AG. In the US/Russia relations thread the participants generally agreed that there were contacts between the Trump campaign and Russians. The debate within the thread was about the impact of Russian meddling on the outcome of the presidential election and what should be done about it.

Similar discussions and debates occurred on television news channels and talk radio, and probably over dinner tables and at coffee houses all across the US. There was nothing unique about the subject matter of the issue-oriented threads. What was unique was that it took place on a private citizen's Facebook page.

Despite the initial reluctance expressed by a majority of the friends who responded to my original post, 63 people participated in the issue-oriented discussions. Only a few of the participants know each other offline. They were from all demographic categories of age, gender, race, religion, urban/rural, ideology, and political persuasion. They have various levels of education; some only high school and others professional and advanced degrees. Professors and factory workers engaged with each other in the topical discussions. One participant is Bulgarian and lives in London; another lives in India. All of the others were "regular" Americans willing to use Facebook as a medium to engage with their fellow citizens in civil discussions and to debate political issues.

Participants were not paid. They aren't professional pundits or politicians. Each participant, for their own reasons, just decided they wanted to join in a discussion on Facebook about the issues posed.

It's exciting to know that in this era of siloing and political polarization that such a cross-section of citizens want to participate in dialogue about divisive issues. It's a hopeful sign that the experiment proved Facebook can be used as a medium to bring people together to discuss difficult political issues.

The experiment was motivated by a genuine desire to find out whether Facebook could be used as a medium for civil and rational discourse about political issues among a random group of friends. I wanted to find out whether "regular" people, not pundits, politicians, or paid experts, would be willing to engage with each other that way. I was hopeful they would, but I certainly wasn't sure.

Several friends expressed privately to me that they didn't think it would work and were pleasantly surprised that the experiment succeeded. A few left comments expressing hope that communications about politics might become more open and tolerant. Others expressed doubt that would occur. An example of one of the skeptical comments:

> I would write some civil discourse but I am too busy selling houses since Trump got elected. Keep me in the loop. I am not sure that civil discourse can happen on Facebook or any other social media, particularly Twitter which I find lethal, but what a great topic for a book... I fear however in the short synopsis here, that liberal arts schools are moving away from useful discourse. What I valued most from my liberal arts education is the fact that it taught me to look at other viewpoints and take them seriously and discuss... That liberal arts education made me a critical thinker... People think that is elementary. However as I go through life those skills are not that

simple to attain it appears. So to sum up what I think is lacking in many of our workers who are applying for jobs today is the ability to read, write and apply critical thinking skills. This would actually also apply to people who post on Facebook. Wanted to make sure I tied in the objective of your original post.

I casually knew M_ in college but had no contact with her for decades. She wasn't in my FB friends list when she posted her comment. She was a friend of a friend. My page is open for comments by friends of friends. We friended each other after she posted her comment.

It was interesting that M_ brought up the importance of a liberal arts education in developing critical skills necessary to engage in rational discourse. For decades the number of students majoring in liberal arts has fallen while Business and STEM enrollment has increased. Students are told that the jobs are in technology, and kids with debt need jobs, so they choose their majors accordingly. Universities know what butters their bread. So, when donors and the government want to fund engineering, IT, and business programs rather than liberal arts, what choice do administrators have?

As a Humanities major who loved his liberal arts education, universities deemphasizing liberal arts grieves me. I think M_ may be on to something by relating the decline of interest in liberal arts to the coarsening of our public discourse. How this relates to a plea for greater civility in political discussions is encapsulated in the response to an interviewer's question given by Martha Nussbaum, an eminent professor of philosophy at the University of Chicago. Ms. Nussbaum was talking about a class she teaches in the Law School.

But we also need debate across political positions. I sought out a junior colleague, who's our most conservative faculty member in the law school, to teach with me. The topic was public morality and legal conservatism, and we started by reading people like Edmund Burke and then John Stuart Mill, James Fitzjames Stephen, the Hart-Devlin debate, and then we moved up to present-day issues like sex laws, prostitution, pornography, and drug laws.

We have some really excellent students who have very conservative religious views. (I have religious views too, but they are not conservative.) And we had these amazing debates where people would actually say, Well, I think we should reintroduce sodomy laws to strengthen the traditional family. And instead of that person being hurled into outer darkness, there was actually a respectful debate, in which another student said, Well, I'm a gay man from a southern Baptist family, and I want to tell you there's a lot in what Hart says about the psychic cost of repression. So, they heard each other.

I think that's what we really need in America, for people to hear each other.
"Martha C. Nussbaum Talks About the Humanities, Mythmaking, and International Development," The 2017 Jefferson Lecturer in Conversation with NEH Chairman William D. Adams, HUMANITIES, Spring 2017, Volume 38, Number 2

That kind of dialogue among students and teachers occurs every day all across the offline world in high school, college, and grad school classrooms. If we can do it in the classroom, we can do it on Facebook.

My new-old friend M_ yearns for a public that is informed and thinks critically. But she's skeptical social media can positively contribute to those civic goals. It won't, if we don't try. My reply to her comment was:

I'm not so pessimistic about what's happening in classrooms as you, M_. My experience teaching at Marian & Butler reaffirmed my faith in the ability of current students to think critically. But I am disappointed that FB does not more often rise to the level of its highest & best use. It can be used for reasoned argument & civil discourse. We FB users have just chosen more often to use it to vent or for blather.

Imagine how much more productive we could be in human relations, if we were able to better master our fight or flight response. If we did not respond to disagreement and argument as if it endangered us, work, play, and love relations would improve. Primitive instincts served primitives well in their physically dangerous environment. They serve us less well, especially within the 21st Century environment of social media.

I summed up my own response to the entire experiment with this post:

I would like to wind up this experiment of trying to encourage civil discourse on FB about tough political issues by thanking all of you who have participated. I plan to write an article (maybe a book) addressing the question of whether civil conversation can take place on FB. These conversations are proof that it is possible. It's tempting to use social media either to shout your own opinions and insult those who oppose you. Or, to huddle only with like minded friends, so you're never challenged by reasonable views different from your own. Yet, most of us agree that growth comes from exposure to new & different information, interpretations, analysis, and conclusions. I think we don't use social media to its full potential when we hide from opposing opinions or just attack those with whom we disagree. I'll let you know what develops with my writing project.

# Afterword

*A Mission for Depolarization and Moderation*

"I can think of no one objection that will possibly be raised against this proposal..."
Johnathan Swift, *A Modest Proposal*

I do not claim the mantle of an "influence leader" who can spread positive change through an extensive social network, like Nicholas Christakis urged in his TED Talk. What I did hope to accomplish was to show my FB friends that they can communicate as rational and respectful adults on Facebook with people who have opposing political views from their own. I hope this understanding spreads beyond my network and will play a modest part in reducing the unhealthy temperature of our body politic.

A key to creating a civil culture within the discussion threads was making the request for civility and an occasional reminder to be respectful. My FB experiment is evidence that "habituating depolarization", the way it's encouraged by Better Angels, can work on Facebook, not just in face-to-face encounters. Simply requesting people to be civil and respectful creates a group dynamic that promotes courtesy and peer pressure that reinforces the expectation of civility.

I didn't give up posting about political issues after declaring the experiment at an end. Since then I've intermittently put up posts on political issues and asked for comments. In the weeks following the declared end of the experiment I posted questions about US intervention in Syria, proposed budget cuts in science research and the arts, the extent to which US presidents have an obligation to be truthful, deficit spending by the federal government, reactions to President Trump's release of classified information to Russians, the US's withdrawal from the Paris Climate Accord, etc.

A friend who participated in the experiment began a thread concerning the Trump/Ryan attempt to "repeal and replace" the Affordable Care Act. His post generated a lot of heat, but commenters were civil to each other without a reminder that they should be. In each of the post-experiment threads I started there were passionate comments and some angry-toned rebuttals, but no ad hominem attacks. Perhaps the habit of civility had formed among some of my FB friends.

In the post-experiment threads there were nasty remarks about both Obama and Trump, as there were in comments posted during the experiment. Some of these disparaging comments were disrespectful of Trump and Obama. But those men are public figures, not fellow participants in the thread. As long as a comment about a politician is not just ugly and mean for the sake of being ugly and mean, it should be considered within the bounds of civil discourse on Facebook.

Criticizing and making fun of our political representatives is one of the great traditions of democratic republics dating back to the Greek comic playwright Aristophanes. It's most effective when done artfully. Unfortunately, most of the attacks on the person of politicians I've seen in social media are inartful and just mean-spirited.

Responding to a political leader's personality and character, positively or negatively, is an essential aspect of democracy. We should care about personal traits, like integrity, in our leaders.

Most Americans rank Bill Clinton's performance as President positively, but his ability to govern was compromised by the bill of impeachment against him. Even if you think his sexual affairs were irrelevant to his competence in governing, you have to admit that he had character flaws which had an adverse effect on his ability to govern and his legacy. The repercussions of his dishonesty, infidelity, and mistreatment of women rippled out beyond his own presidency. The negative reaction of the public to his infidelity was a factor, I think, in Al Gore's loss to George W. Bush. Trump's campaign used Bill's sexual transgressions, I think somewhat successfully, as a weapon against Hillary.

Fans of the Clintons may think tarring Hillary with Bill's indiscretions, or even factoring that in to a judgment on Bill's presidential performance, is unfair. Trump supporters apparently didn't rank his misogynistic behavior as a significant factor in their judgment of his fitness to serve as President. His opponents did. The reality is we do care about character, especially in "the other guy". So it has to be fair game in political discourse.

I started a post-experiment thread questioning the advisability of the US launching 59 Tomahawk cruise missiles against a Syrian airbase on April 6, 2017. The missile strike was President Trump's response to the alleged use of poison gas on Syrian civilians by the Assad regime. The responses to my post divided strictly along pro and anti Trump lines, as had most of the comments during the experimental phase. Some were pretty aggressive and passionate. But again, no personal attacks were launched among commenters.

44 comments or replies were posted, and only one used excessive capital letters.

IF WE DON'T TAKE THIS MONSTER OUT WE SHOULD APOLOGIZE TO IRAQ. THIS CLOWN MUST GO. CONGRATS MR PRESIDENT FOR DOING WHAT THE LAST COWARD WOULD NOT.

Another mocked President Trump by posting an all-caps tweet of Trump's when Obama was President.

I like a president who tweets in all caps. Shows strength. Donald J. Trump on Twitter "AGAIN, TO OUR VERY FOOLISH LEADER, DO NOT ATTACK SYRIA - IF YOU DO MANY VERY BAD THINGS...

So yes, there were snarky and sarcastic comments and a few that simply stated a pro or anti Trump stance. Examples:

He did the right thing, something that should have been done before.

No worries. That bomb attack really scared the bejeebers out of Assad.

But most of the comments, same as during the experimental stage, were thoughtful and reasoned.

I have to admit that, as time passed after ending the experiment, my own habit of being conscientiously civil and respectful waned somewhat. I put up a post which was not posed as a neutral question inviting comments on both sides of an issue. Rather, it was a provocative statement. It was inspired by what a high school teacher told me about his discussion with a student.

Jeff Rasley April 5 at 11:15am. A teacher-friend recently described a conversation with a student in which the student argued that the US government was just as repressive as those which follow Sharia (some version) Law. I suggested the teacher ask the student to consider how many women in the US are demanding to be forcibly veiled or want to be prohibited from driving a car. I also suggested the student ask LGBT friends whether they would like to be imprisoned for expressing their sexuality. The US is far from perfect, but there are not a lot of Americans fleeing our shores to emigrate to Saudi Arabia, Iran, or "the Islamic State".

(This photo accompanied the post)

Many of the same friends who participated in the experimental threads commented. One sub-thread devolved into an argument over whether Christians were just as guilty as Muslims in perpetrating terrorism and atrocities.

I've participated in a number of offline discussions along those lines, and I should have anticipated that's where this FB post would go. In every discussion of this sort I've witnessed, liberals feel an instinctive need to passionately argue that Christianity has been as bad, and maybe worse, than Islam in inspiring violent-inhumane actions. They position themselves as defending the majority of innocent Muslims. Conservatives argue that currently Muslims are much more likely to perpetrate terrorism than Christians. And they argue that Muslim-majority countries are more likely to violate human rights than Christian-majority countries.

The thread did not degenerate into name-calling, but it came closer than any of the topical posts in the experiment or any of the other posts about political issues I put up post-experiment. Examples:

You deliberately misrepresent my view. But fine. You are seeing what you want to see.

... why post this on Facebook, other than to generate a frankly masturbatory, self-congratulatory conversation about how great we are compared to Those People--which is exactly what you got. ...

I find the rah rah patriots very limited in their perspective, which is all I have been saying in this entire thread...

An accusation of deliberate misrepresentation and labeling my purpose of posting the anecdote as masturbatory self-congratulation might be considered personally insulting. The boundaries of civility were pushed. But, the middle comment makes a valid point and offers a lesson. If you want to invite conversation or debate about an issue, the topic should be introduced as a question. If the "host" of the discussion takes a side or stakes out a position in the original post, the thread is more likely to incur the ire of friends with opposing views.

Better Angels makes the point in its literature that the facilitator of a discussion group of people with opposing political perspectives should remain neutral. Anyone who has gone through mediation training, or experienced mediation, knows this. If you're going to moderate, don't debate. But that was not what I wanted to do with the post about the student telling his teacher that the US is as repressive as countries with Sharia law. I wanted to blow off a little steam about what I considered a ridiculously inaccurate statement by a high school student.

I don't think it's inappropriate to use social media to do that. But, if we do, we are likely to generate heated replies like those above. As pointed out in the third comment above, you'll get "rah rah responses" by those that agree with you, but you'll get blasted by friends that disagree with you. If your purpose is to receive rah rah affirmation, then you should join a like-minded group and limit your one-sided posts to the protected circle of that group. But then we're back to the problem of siloing. And really, what is accomplished by posting political statements you know the members of your private group will agree with. Nothing is learned. No one has to think seriously to develop a cogent argument in response. It is just a FB circle jerk.

What I did in the experiment (and the other post-experiment discussion threads) was to introduce a topic as a neutral question. But after the discussion got going, I would participate as a commenter with my own point of view. I advocated for moderate-pragmatic solutions to the issues discussed. When I was ready to wind up the discussion I tried to summarize the points made without tipping the scale to my side of the argument.

I do think the method I developed is the highest and best use of Facebook on a political/civic level. When it's used for civil conversation and the development of thoughtful arguments about important issues, Facebook does serve the laudatory purposes outlined by Mark Zuckerberg in his April 2015 post.

Several friends affirmed that conclusion in messages to me. The fact that follow-up posts on political topics generated continued interest is evidence that others found the project worthwhile. On the other hand, two friends that were regular contributors from the Lib-Dem side reached the end of their patience by the time I posted a question about President Trump disclosing classified information to Russia. They informed me they would no longer participate in any future posts. This is the explanation one of them gave:

> Sorry Jeff Rasley, I just can't participate in these things anymore. I get so angry and frustrated that I end up blocking the people you want me to interact with. If a person "believes" $2 + 2 = 5$, then explaining to him/her that $2 + 2$ actually $= 4$ will have no effect. Even if you SHOW them by counting on your fingers ("How do you KNOW you're showing me 4 fingers? BECAUSE SOMEBODY TOLD YOU THAT WAS 4 FINGERS, BUT THEY LIED! THAT IS ACTUALLY 5 FINGERS!")... At this point, I think anyone capable of being swayed by argument has already been swayed, so that what is left are "True Believers" that can never be swayed from their belief...

My response:

> The purpose of asking what people think and why they think it is not to change minds. It is to find out what they think and why. Why get angry, because someone disagrees with you or even sees reality completely different? You're only responsible for your own feelings and thoughts, not theirs. But, if you don't interact with people "on the other side", you will remain ignorant of them and there never will be a possibility of finding any common ground.

(I think Daryl Davis would "like" that reply if he was a FB friend.)

This friend decided pro-Trump people are not worth communicating with. Why? Because they are so illogical they refuse to agree with me. Because they do not see reality the way I do. I am right. They are wrong. End of story.

The common theme that emerged in my conversations, online and offline, with anti-Trumpers as to why they don't want to engage with pro-Trumpers is that pro-Trumpers are malicious, stupid, or both. The modern Christian martyr Dietrich Bonhoeffer, who was executed for plotting against Hitler, had this to say about malice and stupidity:

> Stupidity is a more dangerous enemy of the good than malice. One may protest against evil; it can be exposed and, if need be, prevented by use of force. Evil always carries within itself the germ of its own subversion in that it leaves behind in human beings at least a sense of unease. Against stupidity we are defenseless. Neither protests nor the use of force accomplish anything here; reasons fall on deaf ears; facts that contradict one's prejudgment simply need not be believed- in such moments the stupid person even becomes critical – and when facts are irrefutable they are just pushed aside as inconsequential, as incidental. In all this the stupid person, in contrast to the malicious one, is utterly self-satisfied and, being easily irritated, becomes dangerous by going on the attack. For that reason, greater caution is called for than with a malicious one. Never again will we try to persuade the stupid person with reasons, for it is senseless and dangerous.
> Dietrich Bonhoeffer, **Letters and Papers from Prison**

Bonhoeffer thought Hitler malicious and many of his followers stupid. Some angry Lib-Dems think Trump is malicious and his followers so stupid they are hopeless. If you agree with that assessment, then this project looks like a fool's errand. But, do you really think *all* Trump voters are stupid? I know doctors, lawyers, successful business owners, and professors with PhDs that voted for Trump.

If the goal is to persuade Trump supporters that they are wrong and you are right, there is little hope for achieving that goal. If the goal is the less ambitious one of trying to maintain civil communications and slowly building bridges of trust to find common ground, that is not unachievable.

Isn't it rather malicious and stupid to write off *all* those who disagree with you about who should be President as deplorable?

It is dispiriting that some friends, who actively participated through the experimental phase and beyond, did not learn the value of continued engagement with people "on the other side". I think that in some cases this is due more to psychology than politics or social media use. Intolerance is a personality trait of some people, and it manifests itself in the psychology of extremists on both the right and left. Why would C_ become so furious at people, who have exemplary characters, as to compare them to child molesters just because they voted for Donald Trump? This exchange in a post-experiment thread exemplifies what seems to me the personality trait of intolerance linked to political extremism.

> Jeff Rasley ... here are examples of friends I respect who voted for Trump and have given me coherent reasons for doing so: 1. WWII vet & bronze star awardee, 2. retired doc who gives countless hours of volunteer med treatment, 3. brilliant linguist who retired to devote her life to philanthropy, & 4. builder/mgr. who specialized in Sect. 8 housing for the poor. These friends are not deplorable. One told me she "never approved of Trump", but she thinks Hillary would have continued "the drift toward socialism", which she thinks will ultimately not serve us well. These are debatable issues about which reasonable friends can disagree. But, if we think contemptuously of everyone we disagree with, we have lost an important civilizing value -- tolerance. May 25 at 5:08pm

> C_ ... I wouldn't be friends with 45 because of his actions and I have no interest in being friends with those who support his actions. I have no internal curiosity to understand their motivation nor the need to feel fair and balanced. I am 59 years old and have earned my right to be opinionated. I am not at all embarrassed by or ashamed of it. I'm tolerant of a whole lot of things. Child molesters and Trump supporters are not among them. May 25 at 10:25pm

Yet, C_ was one of the most active participants in the threads. So, while she excoriated pro-Trumpers in many of her posts, she was not uncivil to any particular pro-Trump participants. Her disparagement of Trump supporters was in general, not toward specific individuals.

131

The most surprising development with C_ on Facebook was that in early June of 2017 she began a discussion thread about the fairness of criminal sentencing. She took a strong and argumentative stance within the discussion, but she opened it with a neutral question. One of the commenters, who had participated in the experiment, noted that C_ was engaged in what "Jeff Rasley has been trying as an experiment about getting people on the right and the left to talk to each other."

Unhealthy polarization within our body politic will obviously require treatment beyond encouraging interaction on Facebook. However, that C_, who is still furious at Trump supporters, would model my method of promoting civil engagement on Facebook is a signal that hope for reducing animosity across the political divide is not in vain. My little experiment is a flickering candle of hopefulness that civil discussions will increase as we get further away from the heat of the 2016 Presidential Election.

Now, I need to point out that most of my 680 FB friends completely ignored the project. Only 63, just under one-tenth of the total, participated at all. (More friends did join in the post-experiment discussions.)

A few weeks after the experiment officially ended, I initiated a couple threads about favorite music groups and pop songs. Over 100 friends participated; far more than the total number that posted in the experimental threads.

One friend commented that she preferred this sort of post to political ones. Understandable. There were many different answers to the questions posed about best tunes and favorite groups. But commenters didn't actually argue or even disagree directly with each other. No emotional heat or angry passion was expressed. The Beatles won the popularity contest by a landslide. A friend's comment in favor of Nat King Cole and "the Mormon Choir" was politely ignored. But no one was even mildly criticized for expressing alternative taste in music. No comment even came close to the borderline of civility.

My reply to the friend who preferred the post about favorite music to political issues:

It's certainly more pleasant just to share and not argue. But, in this era of polarization, when people with differing political opinions refuse to talk to each other or just shout angrily, I've made it one of my missions to try to encourage friends with different points of view to engage in civil conversation.

It is tempting to be pessimistic about the likelihood of polarization being reduced and moderation increased in the political sphere. As friend Bob put it, "Irrational discourse and the politics of extremism are going to get worse before they get better." There is a ray of hope that Bob is wrong.

Emmanuel Jean-Michel Frédéric Macron was elected President of France and took office May 14, 2017. His party, République En Marche (Republic Onwards), which is moderate and centrist by European standards, was founded in April 2016, just a year before his election. It won a landslide victory in parliamentary elections, ensuring Macron an overwhelming majority in the National Assembly.

The French electorate rejected the extremist parties on the left and right. The Socialist Party that governed France under the previous administration only received 7.4% of the votes cast in the parliamentary elections. Marine Le Pen, leader of the far-right National Front, was thrashed by Macron in the presidential run-off election by a two-to-one majority of the vote (66.1% to 33.9%). Her party only received 13.5% of the vote in the parliamentary elections. Édouard Philippe, France's prime minister, said after the results were in, "By their vote, the French, in their great majority, preferred hope to anger..."

Voters in the Netherlands also rejected extremism. Geert Wilders, was called "the Dutch Donald Trump". During the campaign he was surging in the polls, and pundits predicted his far-right Freedom Party (PVV) could sweep him into office in a wave of anti-immigrant populist-sentiment similar to the UK's Brexit vote and the Trump victory. Instead, his party only received 13% of the vote in the April 2017 parliamentary elections. The Netherlands will be governed by a coalition of centrist parties.

These recent European elections indicate that the wave of rightwing populism is subsiding. There was already exhaustion with ineffective socialist policies. Instead of turning to the far right or left, European voters seem to be turning to the middle.

The great psychologist of the American psyche, Alexis de Tocqueville, in his mid 19th Century classic, ***Democracy in America***, described the US as a nation of pragmatic materialists, who were also evangelical about their religions.

The position of the Americans is therefore quite exceptional, and it may be believed that no democratic people will ever be placed in a similar one. Their strictly Puritanical origin, their exclusively commercial habits, even the country they inhabit, which seems to divert their minds from the pursuit of science, literature, and the arts, the proximity of Europe, which allows them to neglect these pursuits without relapsing into barbarism, a thousand special causes, of which I have only been able to point out the most important, have singularly concurred to fix the mind of the American upon purely practical objects. His passions, his wants, his education, and everything about him seem to unite in drawing the native of the United States earthward; his religion alone bids him turn, from time to time, a transient and distracted glance to heaven.

Americans have been seduced away from their essentially pragmatic and moderate nature at different times in our history by demagogues exciting crowds with religious-like fervor. In due course we have found our way back to being grounded in practicality. Rather than being cynical and pessimistic, we can help turn ourselves back on course, as our European friends have. Let's start by treating those who stray from the course with civility. And then, work actively for moderate, sensible, pragmatic political solutions and for the candidates who support that approach.

# Postscript

*Impeachment of Donald J. Trump?*

Events leading toward the possible impeachment of President Trump have unfolded so rapidly as I've tried to wind up this writing project, I feel compelled to add a postscript. It might seem out of date by the time you read it.

The drum beat for impeachment of the President grows louder as publication of this book nears. A Facebook friend posted a question asking those of us who live in Indiana, what do we think of Mike Pence as President. My reply was that Pence was not made an offer of employment by the law firm he summer interned for after his second year of law school. I know that because I was on the firm's recruiting committee. I liked Pence. He seemed like a pleasant, khaki-wearing, frat boy sort of fellow to me. However, the higher ups in the firm evaluated him as not having the right stuff to be a top notch lawyer. So, a guy who was deemed not sufficiently smart to be employed as an associate attorney in a medium-large law firm in Indianapolis may be the next President of the United States of America.

So, will Pence be better than Trump? That was what my non-Hoosier FB friend was getting at with her question. I was surprised that Pence became such a hardline-rightwing-Evangelical-Christian-Republican, when he got into politics. It didn't square with the way he came across to me in our admittedly brief encounters when he interned for the law firm. But he proved to be much smarter at politics than he was at impressing partners in a quasi-silk stocking law firm.

Although I didn't see it, Pence does seem convicted in his faith. To those that share his Catholic-Evangelical faith and rightwing politics he should be preferable to Trump. It's pretty clear that Donald Trump doesn't believe in much of anything other than his egoistic need to win. So, Pence is your man, if you want a leader that actually believes in the Evangelical Tea Party vision for America.

So which is better for the country, a narcissist or a true believer?

In Indiana we learned that Pence as Governor endangered the State's economy and the acceptance of same-sex marriage by pushing through his pet bill, Indiana's Religious Freedom Restoration Act (RIFRA). The law was intended to allow businesses to discriminate against gays on religious grounds. However, when the business-dominated state legislature felt the backlash of threatened boycotts from organizations like the NCAA, NBA, and NFL, it backtracked and gutted Pence's prized legislation. Had he not been picked as Trump's VP, polls in Indiana showed Pence was in for a tough fight to get reelected Governor in 2016.

Yet, he remains popular with the Religious Right. A fellow Hoosier with that political leaning replied to the question about what us Hoosiers think of Pence as President: "I would sleep like a baby at night." P_ voted for Trump, is upset about the rumbles for impeachment, but would be delighted to have Mike Pence in the Oval Office.

P_ and I disagree politically on many issues. We were not friends, but were acquaintances in high school. We connected as friends on Facebook by P_ joining in the experimental discussion threads. We've disagreed civilly on the issues raised in the threads. I appreciated P_'s doggedness in defending President Trump in several of the discussions.

If Trump is impeached, whatever the outcome, it will be even more important that people like P_ and me are able to maintain civil lines of communication. Whether they like Pence or not, many Trump supporters will be furious if their man is impeached, just as Bill Clinton's supporters were.

The case for impeachment of Trump is quite different than it was for President Clinton. If Trump is impeached it will likely be for collusion with a foreign adversary or obstruction of justice in trying to hinder the investigation of collusion with that same adversary, Putin's Russia. These charges would be more like Watergate than Monica-gate.

After Nixon resigned in disgrace, because he was about to be impeached and the evidence was incontrovertible that he had acted with felonious intent, I had an encounter I will never forget. Ed lived down the street from my boyhood home. He was over 70 and a life-long conservative Republican. I was home from college the summer of 1974 during the Watergate hearings. I saw Ed walking down our street, and stopped to greet him. He shook his head, looked me in the eye and said, "That god damn Nixon betrayed me, and I'll never vote for a Republican again."

I was stunned and impressed. At first, it seemed like an over-reaction on Ed's part. My father, also a life-long Republican, tried to elaborate on how betrayed Nixon supporters felt. He explained that they felt like Nixon had lied to them personally.

In the next presidential election some of the felt-betrayed Republicans voted for Jimmy Carter. Nixon's Vice-President, Gerald Ford, pardoned Nixon after Ford assumed the presidency following Nixon's resignation. The pardon was another cut into the lacerated skin of betrayed voters, and they took it out on Ford in the polls. Turncoat Republicans may have later regretted it and voted for Ronald Reagan to oust Carter. But still, the Democrats had an opportunity to swing some votes their way after the Watergate debacle, and they did.

Some disappointed Republicans, like Ed, may have turned away from politics or turned to even darker forces on the far right. The John Birch Society had members in my hometown of Goshen, Indiana, and I wondered if Ed might have found shelter there.

If Trump is impeached, I worry that enraged Trump supporters might turn to darker forces on the extreme right rather than to traditional Republican-conservative or moderate politics. Some of my Progressive-Democrat friends will gloat. I don't blame them in the sense that I thought all along that Trump was a very poor choice by the Repubs. Rather than gloat, I would like to keep the lines of communication open. That will not be possible if anti-Trumpers dominate discussions in the public press and social media with, "I told you so, stupid!" If contempt for Trump supporters, as expressed in this comment in a post-experiment thread is typical, Trump supporters may feel that they will only be welcome in even more extreme rightwing silos.

> U sound so benevolent! I do not agree with or respect the opinion of Trump and crew! He's a lying, cheating, con and if that's what you respect I feel sorry for you!!!

This comment was in response to a post in which I thanked friends for participating in the experiment. Just indicating appreciation for people on both sides of the political divide was so offensive to this anti-Trumper that she was driven to three exclamation marks of pity for my poor soul.

After James Comey was fired from his position as FBI Director and it was clear that Trump was trying to derail the investigation into collusion between his campaign and the Russians, an anti-Trump friend remarked to me that, "Anyone who still supports Trump ought to lose their right to vote!" She did not mean it facetiously.

Again, I understand the anger in the sense that I too thought Trump was obviously unfit to be President. As events have unfolded in the early days of his presidency there is little evidence to support a change of that opinion. But it is disturbing that progressive liberals, who are so sensitive about issues of social justice, have such hatred toward Trump supporters that they would like to deny them the right to vote. Would these

"Progressives" also discriminate against Trump supporters in housing and employment?

This sort of illiberal attitude by liberals was criticized by the liberal CNN commentator Fareed Zakaria in a May 28, 2017 broadcast. His point was that true liberalism accepts and respects the right of disagreement within civilized bounds. No matter how convinced we were of his unfitness and how strongly we favor impeachment, it is illiberal to condemn someone merely for their support of Trump. Condemn Trump, not his supporters. It will be more productive of restoring civility in political discussions to invite them in. The Democrats might even pick up some disenchanted Trumpers, like Carter did with disillusioned Nixon voters. But that will depend on Democrats treating former Trump-voters civilly, rather than despising them.

Disturbing statistics about the loss of faith in democracy and a willingness to turn to authoritarian rule are compiled by Roberto Stefan Foa and Yascha Mounk in "The Democratic Disconnect," *Journal of Democracy*, July 2016. The authors found that "world values surveys" since World War II reveal a trend of increasing cynicism about the value of political participation in Western democratic countries. Millennials are the most disillusioned generation in the modern era about democracy, since polling data has been compiled. 26% do not think "free and fair elections" are important, according to one of the surveys described by Foa and Mounk. The authors sound this warning about the erosion of faith in democracy:

> If we take the number of people who claim to endorse democracy at face value, no regime type in the history of mankind has held such universal and global appeal as democracy does today. Yet the reality of
> contemporary democracies looks rather less triumphant than this fact might suggest. Citizens of democracies are less and less content with their institutions; they are more and more willing to jettison institutions
> and norms that have traditionally been regarded as central components
> of democracy; and they are increasingly attracted to alternative regime forms.

The decline in the commitment to democratic values is related to an increasing feeling of powerlessness and anger among Americans. The anger and recrimination of the electorate manifested during and after the 2016 campaign reflects more of a hatred for the other side than loyalty to our side. The inclination is to lash out rather than produce rational arguments to support what our party and candidates stand for. That was the way both the Trump and Clinton campaigns were run, and too many of us have followed their leads.

The week I was finishing the final draft of this book was the week of June 2017 when a deranged gunman, James Hodgkinson, opened fire at a baseball diamond in Alexandria, Virginia, during a practice of the Republican baseball team for the annual Congressional charity ball game. Five people were wounded, including two Capitol Police officers, a congressional staffer, and a lobbyist. House majority whip Steve Scalise was shot in the hip. His wound was the most serious. The shooter was killed by the police. Hodgkinson was a leftist political-activist and a Bernie Sanders campaign volunteer. His apparent motive was to kill Republicans.

> Hodgkinson had a history of violent behavior, and his social feed was a dark parody of the dismal state of the nation's political discourse, where disagreement is personal and anger is visceral. He had joined groups called Terminate the Republican Party and The Road to Hell Is Paved With Republicans.
>
> In this way, Hodgkinson was just another symptom of a creeping national disease. Rarely a week goes by these days without new evidence that the debate over ideas and policy is giving way to violence. Opposing protesters attack one another from the streets of St. Paul or Berkeley. A soon-to-be elected Congressman in Montana body-slammed a reporter for asking an unwelcome question the day before the election. Vile comments once considered unfit for public discourse are common currency online.
>
> Most days, partisans benefit by stoking the political outrage. But few in Washington now doubt that anger has gone too far, crossing from passion to danger, from appropriate to irrational. "This has to stop," said Illinois Republican Rodney Davis, still dressed in his baseball uniform and cleats, when he returned to the U.S. Capitol. "And it has to stop today."
> Michael Scherer, *Time*, "The Virginia Shooting and America's Creeping National Disease," Jun 14, 2017 (online)

So what can we as individual citizens do to stop the "creeping national disease" of extreme polarization and loss of democratic values?

If we leave it up to the PACs and politicians to take the lead, it might get worse rather than better. Launching attacks or siloing in social media is not the thing that's going to help reverse the trend. Fighting and hiding will more likely deepen cynicism, pessimism, or complacency about our traditional-liberal democratic values.

Rather than use social media in the vile way James Hodgkinson did, we can engage with it for higher and better purposes. It's a tool that didn't exist for previous generations of voters. If we use it effectively, we can have an impact on what the politicians do. Barack Obama was the first presidential candidate to use email as a primary means of communicating with voters. He won. Donald Trump used Twitter, and he won. Instead of using Facebook to bash political opponents, let's hash out disagreements and possibly find some common ground on important issues. We can at least develop a better understanding through civil conversation of what divides us and why. That would lower the temperature of our body politic so more moderate voices could be heard as an alternative to the shrieking of angry extremists.

The value of civil discussion on Facebook need not end there. After we've vetted our own opinions and arguments, we'll have a firmer grasp of the relevant facts and better understanding of the issues. Then, we should move past the point of discussion to encourage activism by calling out politicians who behave undemocratically and do not act for the greater good of the country. We can ask everyone we communicate with on Facebook to join in political discussions but also to march, demonstrate, petition, call legislators, and vote for the best candidate.

My commitment is to urge us all toward moderation and good will toward fellow citizens. If we can set aside unworthy emotions that deepen our political divide, concentrate on finding solutions to the problems our country and communities face, we can then work toward a brighter future with less rancor but firm in our purpose.

Or, we can feed our primitive fight or flight impulse by lashing out in social media and then duck into our silos. If we do that, the unhealthy polarization of the time of Trump will get even worse.

# About the Author

Jeff Rasley is the author of ten books, including *Polarized; the Case for Civility in the Time of Trump*. He has published numerous articles in academic and mainstream periodicals, including Newsweek, Chicago Magazine, ABA Journal, Family Law Review, and Friends Journal

Rasley has engaged in social activism and philanthropic efforts from an early age. In high school he co-founded the Goshen Walk for Hunger. In law school he was an advocate for renters' rights as the leader of the first rent strike in Indiana, and he served as a lobbyist and president of the Indianapolis Tenants Association. As an attorney for Legal Services organization he was lead counsel on two class action suits on behalf of prisoners which resulted in judgments requiring the construction of two new jails in Central Indiana. Jeff was the lead plaintiff in a class action requiring the clean-up of the White River after it was polluted by an industrial chemical spill. Jeff is the founder of the Basa Village Foundation, which raises money for culturally sensitive development work in the Basa area of Nepal. He currently serves as an officer or director for six nonprofit corporations.

Jeff is a graduate of the University of Chicago, A.B. magna cum laude, Phi Beta Kappa, All-Academic All-State Football Team and letter winner in swimming and football; Indiana University School of Law, J.D. cum laude, Moot Court and Indiana Law Review; Christian Theological Seminary, M.Div. magna cum laude, co-valedictorian and Faculty Award Scholar. He was admitted to the Indiana, U.S. District Court, and U.S. Supreme Court Bars.

He is married to Alicia Rasley, an English professor and the author of historical romances and writing craft books. Alicia is a RITA Award winner and her novel *The Year She Fell* was an Amazon-Kindle best-seller.

Author above Kyanjin Gompa, Langtang, Nepal

Made in the USA
Middletown, DE
18 September 2018